A Season in Hell

BY PERCY KNAUTH

Percy Knauth

HARPER & ROW, PUBLISHERS

1817

A Season in Hell

NEW YORK, EVANSTON, SAN FRANCISCO, LONDON

Grateful acknowledgment is made for permission to reprint an excerpt from "War Song" from *The Portable Dorothy Parker,* Copyright 1944 by Dorothy Parker, Copyright renewed 1972 by Lillian Hellman. Originally appeared in *The New Yorker.* Reprinted by permission of The Viking Press, Inc.

FIRST EDITION

Designed by Dorothy Schmiderer

Library of Congress Cataloging in Publication Data

Knauth, Percy, 1914–
    A season in hell.

    1. Depression, Mental—Personal narratives.
2. Knauth, Percy, 1914–   I. Title.
RC537.K58 1975   616.8'9   74–1826
ISBN 0–06–012421–0

To my children, and to my wife, Behri

A Season in Hell

1

Just after dawn on an April morning not long ago, I, Percy Knauth—free-lance writer, successful editor, veteran of twenty-eight years of overseas reporting, writing and editing for *Time, Life, Sports Illustrated* and, most recently, Time-Life Books; foreign correspondent for the New York *Times* in Berlin, Germany, before that, and assistant to Sigrid Schultz in the Berlin office of the Chicago *Tribune* before *that*—lying in a little attic room high above West Sixty-seventh Street in New York City, decided to kill myself.

It was not a hasty decision. I had thought about it many times. The spare, small room in which I had just awakened was filled with reminders of the many reasons why I had to go on living, but I had put them behind me now. My wife of nearly twenty years lay sleeping gently beside me. A photograph of our two children, a boy and a girl, looked gravely down at me from the wall. On the shelves were books I had written, and on the desk scattered notes and outlines for more books yet to come. There was a small painting of our house in Connecticut in a village by the sea. There were many reasons why I should want to live.

And yet I lay there coolly planning my suicide. I would do it this coming night. The pills lay ready to hand in a small bottle on the table beside my bed. In a few hours I would swallow them, *all* of them.

Why?

I was suffering from a disease. Not cancer, not incurable, it was not even physically painful. Yet I was being poisoned. My life had turned inside out so that everything I saw was a photographic negative. Where there should have been joy, I could feel only an unending sadness. Where I should have felt hope, there was only despair. Where life with its continuing promise should have sustained me, only the oblivion of death attracted me now, for living had become a hell on earth.

My illness was depression.

Beside me in the attic room my wife slept peacefully. I had not known peace for months. Day and night I was swept by fears and agonies that left me reeling.

I ached for sleep. Would I ever know restful sleep again? Even pills gave me only restless snatches in which I tossed and trembled, racked by doubts and horrors that surfaced from my unconscious mind. And always I awoke in the darkest hours, just before dawn.

I had been trying for so long in vain to regain control of my waking mind that I doubted whether I could ever again function as a rational man. The only consistent thoughts I could muster—and sometimes these hammered at me for hours—had to do with words, the tools of my profession, and the proper use of them. One gripped me now. The family name of the aardvark: was it "tubulidentata" or "tubulidentadidae"? I worried about it endlessly, yet could not let it go.

The world, I was sure, had no further use for me, nor had I anything to offer it. When I tried to find strength and comfort in things I had done, I found myself walking down ruined avenues between shattered houses on whose walls bits and pieces of remembered experience flashed briefly into focus and out again, like slides in a psychedelic picture show. I could not control these fragments of memory at all.

And how they came! They were like emissaries from a long-dead past, nightmarish terrors and a dreadful parade of real and imagined shortcomings. The fears of a terror-stricken small boy running through ghostly shaded woods above a black and bottomless lake; the despair of an adolescent youth at boarding school longing for the safety of a home he was sure had been left behind forever; the panic of a man facing wartime combat; the horror of a husband and father trying to cope with the realization that his wife had left him for another man; the nightmare of being alone in the world without a job. All these fears, fought down and rationalized through fifty-seven years of painful—but also often exuberant—living, came back at me now, mercilessly.

Some part of my mind that was still rational was aware that this was nonsense. But awareness made no difference; it was too late. I had passed the point of no return; death was my only escape.

And oddly enough, the thought was comforting. On this rainy April dawn I was not frightened by the prospect of dying. It seemed an entirely logical act, a simple reversal of the process that had brought me into the world some fifty-seven years before. Out of the warmth and darkness into the cold, white day I had come in a swift and brutal transition; all I wanted now was to ease back into the warmth and darkness again. The means were at hand: enough pills to put me to sleep forever.

What I needed first was to get through this final day. I had somehow to persuade my wife to go home to Connecticut and leave me behind; then I could take the pills and still my dread forever. The thought was so seductive in its promise of the peace I yearned for that it broke down all the barriers I had for so long been building against it and left me sobbing helplessly.

Beside me, my wife stirred, then reached out a groping hand. She felt my shaking shoulders and suddenly came wide awake. I lifted my head and for the first time she saw my face as it had looked through all those solitary nights of recent months when I had fought alone in this attic room, away from her and our children because of the work that kept me in New York. Without a word, she took my head into her arms and rocked it on her breast while my tears flowed on and on until it seemed my soul was pouring out through my eyes.

That is the moment that I have to thank for the fact that I am still alive—that moment when I was cradled and comforted like the helpless infant I had become.

2

What had happened to get me to the point where I wanted only to die? I am not, at heart, moody and pessimistic; on the contrary, through most of the years of an eventful life I have always nourished an active joy in the fact of being alive. I have always been eager to get at all the things that were there for my doing, and found 5 peace and satisfaction in doing a job well. Yet all this had now dissolved away. It was as though some silent dark force had pulled the plug out of my life and let the vital juices drain away until I was an empty shell.

When I think back now over that terrible time, it seems to me that for long periods I was living in an entirely different world. There was a real world all around me, but I seldom saw it. I walked familiar streets in the lovely Connecticut village where I lived, but I saw no friendly houses and heard no children's cries; there was only the echo of my own footsteps in an empty gloom. Even the sea, beating in restless rhythm against the breakwater, stretching away in ranks of blue or gray or whitecapped waves toward Europe, seemed a desolate wasteland to me, a repository of whitened bones and blasted hopes.

The sea gave the basic rhythm to our lives out there, but all I heard was the measured drumbeat of death. Each morning when I drew the curtains of our top-floor bedroom window, I looked out upon it to form a judgment of the coming day; but why was it always gray and stormy now?

I was isolated in the world in which I now spent so much of my time, as fully as if I were in solitary confinement in some foreign prison, guarded by men whom I could neither speak to nor understand. It was like dreaming yet being awake, knowing that the dream was real. If I spoke to others, I knew they would not understand me. Instead of forming words, I sensed my mouth making only the "wah-wah" sounds of a nightmare.

I never awoke from this nightmare; it was the only reality I knew. I remember one night in New York when I sweated in the grip of a dream so horrible that I finally forced myself back to consciousness—only to find myself in a strange place filled with stupefying terrors. White light streamed through an open window, cleaving black shadows, and in that light a dim but awful phantom moved—a *white* shadow, hideous to look at, its ghostly shape coming toward me, mouthing incomprehensible, sinister sounds. It came closer and closer until I saw it was—my son! His face was white, his hair was white and moved like an eerie cloud across his eyes. His eyes! They were not eyes at all, but empty sockets behind his hair, black as night, bottomless as the universe. His fleshless lips were breathing a soundless call for help that turned inside me like a sword: "Daddy, Daddy, *Daddy!*"

Asleep or awake, fear was always with me in that dreadful time. Looking back on it today, the only comparison I can make with its unremitting horror is to conjure up an image of myself in my airplane, flying suddenly from the warm blue and gold of clear air and sunlight into the foreboding blindness of a cloud. I had learned to fly in my forties, something I had always wanted to do, and I loved it. Yet there was something in flying that I kept like a secret even from myself—an edge of panic at the thought of flying unexpectedly into a cloud.

Though it never happened, it was an experience I knew as well as if I had lived through it many times. Aloft, my cockpit was like a home to me, its instruments neat and tidy before my eyes, the controls strong and steady and secure. Below my white wings the beloved earth floated past, clean and orderly in the green folds of its hills and the smiling blue of its lakes and ponds and rivers and the sea. I loved my home aloft and all the world, and never more than when I was thus balanced, my life entirely in my own hands, between earth and sky.

But then, abruptly, the cloud would come. No possibility of evasion: a towering mountain lay before me, blocking the way to where I had to go. In the wink of an eye I would pass from light to darkness, from warmth to chill, from life to a shroud. Enveloped in the smothering, damp cotton wool that closed in from all sides, I would lose my sense of up and down, of straight flight or turning. My horizon was gone, and suddenly my cozy little home aloft was transformed into an alien place where panic clutched at me. My compass would deny it, but I had the unshakable conviction that I was turning. I would ease the wheel over to meet the imagined turn, pulling it back slightly to compensate for loss of altitude. And now the compass started going crazy. The plane *really* was turning, and climbing as well. The instruments seemed mad—I felt that I was in a dive, although they showed me going crazily up and up. I pulled the wheel back, straining to find level flight again. With a sickening lurch, the airplane lost flying speed. The nose dropped and I slid off on one wing. The engine roared, the needles on the dials spun. Panic seized me. I no longer knew where I was; I grappled for control. The ship plunged earthward in a steep, descending spiral. If I saw the ground at all when I broke out of the cloud, it was as a frenzied, spinning blur, tipped at a crazy angle—an unfamiliar, alien place where within seconds I would dig my grave.

It never happened, it does not need to happen; and even if it does happen, it can be survived. A man learns to live with this kind of fear; it sharpens the senses and keeps the mind alert, and it is, quite simply, a part of flying, just as fear of drowning is a part of life at sea.

But how can a man continue to survive when all of his life, every waking and sleeping moment of it, turns to fear, when *every* step becomes a step into the unknown?

In the world in which I now lived, panic was the dominating force of my existence. Every morning I fought down panic to get out of bed, and from then on it ruled everything I said or did. A simple question—"Daddy, what time is it?"—would send me into a helpless paroxysm of doubt, bewilderment, confusion, guilt. Why was

it asked? Why was I responsible for answering? Where

was I? Why *couldn't* I answer? What *was* the matter with me, that I could not answer a simple question from my child? Look at your watch, you blind and helpless fool—*Look at your watch!*

But time did not exist for me—that was the answer. I was stumbling along in a void, alone, forsaken, coming from nowhere, going nowhere. Today, when I see pictures of people huddled in a hospital mental ward, heads resting on drawn-up knees, arms clutched over their eyes, I feel a terrible stab of kinship and pity for them; I know what it is like. The moment in which the camera caught them has neither beginning nor end. Their only solace is oblivion.

Of course death held no terror for me. It alone could end my meaningless misery. I sought it, yearned for it, and would embrace it if it came.

Death longed for is amazingly easy to find. I had my pills—all I had to do was swallow them. I had a roof I could jump from—it was fourteen floors straight down, and I had contemplated this possibility often. I had also considered that one day I might swim out to sea and there abandon myself to the water that had always fascinated me.

There were so many simple ways to take my life that it seemed almost ridiculous that I should continue this nightmare struggle to go on living.

Then why did I not do it?

Even today, I am not sure I know the answer to that question. Even to try to find it takes me back through those dark days and nights, inward and downward to depths I have never before attempted. Seeking it is really what this book is all about.

3

How did all this begin?

It had begun nine months before on a sunny summer day, in sparkling blue water, off the warm yellow sands of a beach where we had gone to play. There was a fresh salt breeze blowing, the sea crinkled and laughed in a
10   pattern of tiny wavelets, and on the ocean side of the

peninsula where we planned to picnic great solemn swells surged in, crashing in walls of foam. It was a surfers' day, and their boards cut white trails across the marching waves, while far out on the horizon white sails gleamed as yachts leaned over to that lovely ocean wind. Here and there a charter boat rocked gently, its passengers gazing at their fishing lines, silent and absorbed.

Nothing bad could possibly happen on a day like this and as I nosed our boat gently onto the beach to let my family ashore I felt a warm and peaceful sense of coming home. We had been overseas in Paris for four years. We had liked France and enjoyed the very different sort of life it offered. But this was America, where our roots were; this was home, and I felt a satisfaction such as I had not known for many years as I watched the children scampering up the beach toward the ocean on the other side of the dunes. My wife followed after them with the picnic basket in her hand. I took the boat back out a little ways, threw the anchor overboard, paid out line as she drifted slowly shoreward, then snubbed her and made the line fast. When I jumped in to swim ashore, the water was clear and warm and full of lights and shadows. The world was very beautiful and I was glad to be alive.

Some hours later, when the sky was turning pink and orange on the western horizon, we packed up to go home. The tide had come in; the boat was now far from shore. A fringe of cloud was creeping up the sky from the east, sending long white streamers out across the darkening blue. Far, far up there a jet was humming distantly, a tiny arrow with flashing silver wings, outward bound across the sea—perhaps to France. I watched it go, and for the first time since our return felt nothing at the sight: no twinge of nostalgia, no regret for the pleasant life that we had lost there, no apprehension about the uncertainty that lay ahead. I did not even feel a breath of longing for the wide freedom of the sky that I had once known. It was a plane, and that was all.

The children ran into the water and swam out to the boat; my wife and I waited with the picnic basket and the dog. It was farther than they thought, and by the time they reached it and hung on to the anchor line to rest, they were out of breath. I watched them climb aboard, then went into the water myself and started swimming out toward them.

Under the waning sun the water was dark and much colder. A piece of seaweed brushed my leg, and I snatched myself away in a spasm of alarm. I reached the boat, raised my arm to grab the gunwale and threw one leg up to climb aboard. Suddenly, I was flooded by an icy fear. I couldn't make it.

I tried again; my foot fell inches short of the gunwale. The boat had the lines of a Grand Banks dory, with two-foot sides that slanted steeply inward, and there was no place on that slippery surface where my foot could find a purchase. Seeking to find a spot where one leg would hold while I hoisted the other up and over, I scrabbled along the side of the boat like an awkward crab until my breath was whistling in my lungs.

And all the while fear, the fear that I was to come to know so well, spread inside me, weakening my efforts with its icy touch. Finally, exhausted, I stopped to rest and reconsider.

I *had* to get aboard that boat somehow! I was the only one who could raise the anchor, start the engine and get us home. But how? If I couldn't climb the sides, what could I do?

My children watched me, puzzled, not knowing whether to laugh at my antics or be scared by them. My wife, waiting on shore, sensed I was in some difficulty and shouted encouragement. There was no one else on the beach who might have helped me. I lay back in the water and tried to think.

Finally I had an idea. "Hey, Tim!" I shouted to my son. "Throw me a rope!"

He found a length of line, and under my directions cleated it at both ends so that it formed a loop hanging over the side. I got one foot into the loop and heaved to straighten the leg and swing myself up. Instead my foot slid sideways along the boat, I lost my grip on the gunwale and fell back into the water with a splash.

I was now at the edge of panic. I was fifty-seven years old and out of shape physically; was I losing my strength with age? If I kept this up, might I have a stroke or a heart attack and drown? I had never in my life felt old before. Could my legs really be going back on me? In France I had jogged a mile every day before breakfast, and I meant to keep that up here, too. In my youth these legs had carried me to victory in schoolboy sprints, put me on the college track team as a quarter-miler. I had simply never before considered that one day they might want to quit. Was that what was happening now?

No matter; I couldn't *let* it happen. I got my foot firmly on the loop again and rested for a moment before giving it another try. As I lay backward on the water, gazing upward, I looked into the fading sky and the wisps of streaming cloud. They seemed very far away, and very lonely. I looked into the faces of my children, leaning over the gunwale. I sensed their bafflement: what was the matter with Dad? The cold, dark water lapped at me, draining what strength I still had. With a sudden surge, my strength compounded by something very like despair, I tried again.

Again my foot slid sideways. I would not permit it! The muscles of my arms swelled to the cracking point as I heaved at the gunwale to pull myself up. I simply would not allow my limbs to stop moving. I heaved again and got my chest over the gunwale. I forced my leg to straighten; the muscles felt like chewing gum and barely answered the urgent message of my will. I gained 13 another inch or two, but now I was gasping for breath.

At last, I swung my free leg up and over. I felt something pulling hard somewhere in my side; then it let go with a snap like a breaking rubber band. Pain shot down my thigh, but I was too near to stop now; I smothered it with a sheer effort of will. One final heave, and I pulled my body over the gunwale and rolled gasping into the boat.

The exertion left me shaking all over, and when I got to my feet my left side almost caved in. I limped as I walked, with a dragging pain that ran from the small of my back down my left thigh. I felt as though I had aged thirty years. I started the engine, Timothy managed the anchor, we picked up my wife and the dog and then we headed home.

That night I tossed and turned, tormented by vague, wild dreams. The next morning the pain in my side was worse. From hip to ankle the strength had gone from my left leg; unless I kept my mind on it and regularly straightened it before I put my weight on it, the leg collapsed. Once I forgot as I was descending the cellar stairs, narrowly averting a disaster. My arms were full of empty bottles, and I was concentrating on them as I started down. I took one step, onto my right leg; then another onto my left. But my left leg simply wasn't there.

The shock of it was almost as bad as the fall I very nearly had. I sat down on the stairs abruptly, losing a couple of bottles, which bounced down the steps and shattered on the concrete floor. My body was shaking, my heart pounding with the sudden fright—and then, like a light turned on, a memory of something that had happened ten years before appeared in my mind.

I was having lunch at the Harvard Club in New York with my father. He was seventy-six years old, half blind after two cataract operations, but he was a proud man 14 and he still walked straight and tall. I suppose he was as unwilling then to admit any infirmities as I was now. He was animated, his eyes sparkled and he was full of vigorous conversation.

He loved the Harvard Club. It always reminded him of the happiest time he had known in an eventful life that had brought him a good deal of hardship and sorrow. He relished eating there and greeting old friends, some of whom age had treated more harshly than him despite their material success, something he had seldom known. He nodded and smiled to right and left as we walked toward the long buffet table, and his mind was on what awaited us there: Boston baked beans.

"There's no place in the world that makes baked beans like the Harvard Club," he said as he treated himself to a generous plateful. "They cook them slowly, in the crock, all night long, and they make the heartiest meal there is. Not even in Boston do you get them like this." And off he started, plate in hand, looking for a table.

I served myself and followed him. He walked with a studied, steady step—I could almost *feel* him concentrating on holding himself upright and straight—his white head raised and alert as he gazed out across the crowded room. And as he walked, I saw to my consternation that he was leaving behind him a small but dreadful trail of brown baked beans, sliding off a plate that tipped ever more dangerously in his forgotten hands.

I had felt horror and embarrassment for him at the time, and had not known what to do. He was so proud! Now, sitting on the cellar steps almost ten years later, I experienced a sudden rush of agonizing pity, for I realized what had happened. An aging mind can handle just so much. Preoccupied with walking straight, with avoiding things he might bump into, with greeting friends, he never thought of his hands. They clutched the plate; his fingers told him that unconsciously. But I, in my mind's eye, could see his plate tipping just that 15 last little bit which would send all the beans sliding off onto the floor.

I don't want to imagine what that might have done to him, but a waiter—God bless him!—saw his predicament as soon as I, who could not reach him in time. Without a sign that anything was amiss, he took my father by the arm, relieved him of the plate with a deferential word of apology, and steered him to a seat. Carefully he wiped the plate before he set it down before my father, and then, quite unobtrusively, he proceeded to wipe up the trail of spilled beans. The whole thing was done with such grace that it brought tears to my eyes.

My father, beaming, expectant, totally unaware of what catastrophe had almost befallen him, sat awaiting me, his dignity intact.

And here now sat his son, collapsed on the cellar stairs with his arms full of empty wine bottles. How many such near disasters awaited *me*? Would I, in times to come, be able to carry myself with equal dignity and poise in the old age that now appeared to yawn like an abyss before my eyes?

Old, old, old—I was getting old. That day I started a weird, unsettling game of numbers in my head: in only thirteen years I would be seventy—if I lived that long— and thirteen years were nothing at all! Why, thirteen years *before* I was just about to start my pilot training and that was only yesterday! Dear God, in only thirteen years . . .

It didn't help to tell myself that such things were just the foolishness of a mind filled with self-pity. It didn't help to go to the doctor the next day and learn that I had pulled a ligament in my left leg, and was also suffering from something called sciatica, an inflammation of a nerve resulting from overstraining the muscles in the small of my back. It only made things worse to be told that I would have to spend a fortnight lying down, with hot, wet packs around my hip and thigh, before I would be able to walk normally again.

I passed the better part of the next two weeks just that way, lying down, sometimes reading, mostly thinking, while life went on around me. All I remember today of that time is a shadowy room, its curtains drawn against the hot August sun, and the almost unremitting pain that lived in my hip and thigh. My wife came in occasionally to change the hot packs, which burned as they went on. My children visited me from time to time, their voices unnaturally hushed in the presence of an unfamiliar ill father. My thoughts went around and around, back over my life and ahead, fearfully, into an uncertain future. There in that shadowy room, my descent into hell began.

4

Thinking about that shadowy room, I have to try to recapture the context of the time in which I lay there.

We had bought the house three months before, when I was still stationed in Paris but expecting to come home. A generous Time-Life Books Division had flown

my wife and me over for a couple of weeks of house

hunting, and informed me at the same time that the nature of my future work was uncertain because a company-wide economy wave was lopping off many new projects and leaving a lot of senior editorial people wondering what they might be doing next. I decided that this was the moment to take the plunge and go into business for myself, as a free-lance editor and writer. It was something I had wanted to do for years.

Of course, there was a certain amount of apprehension involved in this decision, but there were high expectations, too. I remember, as the whole family arrived at the village in July, pulling our little trailerful of household goods behind us, that I said to the children: "Take a good look now. You'll be calling this place your home town for the rest of your lives!" I was a pretty happy man.

In the house that awaited us down toward the Point there was not yet a stick of furniture. Still to come were tables, chairs, beds, bureaus and all the other things we had used in Paris, now being forwarded in two huge containers. Meanwhile, my wife and I slept on a couple of borrowed cots, the children in their sleeping bags on the floor. And we became steady patrons of a place called Railroad Salvage.

Although neither my wife nor I had been brought up in affluence, or led what might be called settled, routine lives, we had never seen anything to compare with Railroad Salvage—with the possible exception of the Paris flea market where we had shopped for curiosities from time to time. It was a huge, cluttered warehouse up on Route 184 near the New London bridge, and it fairly shrieked its unbelievable bargains to the world. It sold things salvaged from train wrecks, or bankruptcy sales, or fires—any place where goods could be snapped up at a fraction of their value. We never knew from day to day what we might find there, since things came in and went out almost as fast as the customers going through 19 the doors, but there was always something that we needed—and at that time, after nearly four years abroad and with nothing in our new home, we needed just about everything.

I esteem Railroad Salvage highly these days, but I must confess that at that time the place sometimes gave me an unwarranted case of the jitters. It was worlds removed from our accustomed shopping haunts in Paris; I felt we had wandered by mistake into a parody of a department store. If this was to be the kind of place we would be shopping in thenceforth, it was not an encouraging omen for someone just starting out on his own.

Yet we bought some fine things at Railroad Salvage, things that may well have saved the sanity of all of us in those first difficult weeks of settling down in a new place and into a new life. We got some folding beds there—I spent my two weeks in the shadowy room on one of them—and a couple of inflatable yellow plastic armchairs that the children thought were God's personal gift to them, bouncing on them as though they were trampolines. Then we got three more armchairs (at three dollars each), which would have sold for sixty-five dollars apiece if they had had the bases that their Danish makers had originally designed for them (those had been shipped somewhere else and couldn't be found). My wife put the baseless seats on three worn-out Volkswagen tires that we got for nothing from a neighbor who was going to throw them out, and then she disguised the tires with some flowered fabrics she found in a mill end shop. We still have those armchairs, and all our visitors and cocktail guests sit in them. They are marvelous conversation pieces and I wouldn't give them up for anything, but there were moments, back then, when I would eye them speculatively and wonder if we ever would be able to replace them with armchairs from, say, W. & J. Sloane.

Was I developing a problem then, of insecurity? I don't think so—not yet. True, I had deliberately left my economic security, aged and mellowed through almost three decades of constructive work with Time, Incorporated, behind me in New York. True, I was going to have to depend now entirely on my own wits and my own abilities to survive in a world that had always served me with a periodic pay check handed out by a benevolent and powerful organization. I was sensible enough to wonder occasionally where my future pay checks would come from.

Actually, I knew the answer to that one. I had already signed up for a large editing job that was paying me enough to carry us through the coming year. I also had received an offer to write a book when the editing job was done. I had some money, and we owned our home. So there wasn't really anything to worry about—but these were the seeds of the worries that now began to blossom into nightmares as I lay flat on my back in the shadowy room.

If I couldn't even climb aboard my own boat, I thought to myself as I stared at the dust motes dancing in a stray beam of August sunshine, how in the world was I going to make out earning myself a living?

The two things are, of course, entirely unconnected, but my mind was not making sense the way it should have. There was, for example, the fact that for at least two weeks I would be unable to work. Whenever I had been ill before, for close to thirty-five years, there had always been an organization in the background to pick up the tab; sick or well, I still got my pay check. There was the time in September 1944, when I was sick in Rumania with an unidentifiable fever. Not only did my wife continue to receive my pay check; the fact that I was a war correspondent for *Time* and *Life* magazines helped me in what could have been a very unpleasant situation. I was thousands of miles from home, deep in 21

what had only recently been enemy territory, surrounded on all sides by Russian occupation troops, with
no place where I could cash traveler's checks, and I
couldn't even find out what was wrong with me because
I couldn't speak Rumanian. My only link to life was the
United States 14th Air Force, present in Bucharest in
the form of its PRO, Lieutenant Colonel Tex McCrary,
who could call on any one of several B-17 bombers to fly
a sick journalist to Italy, if necessary. Tex McCrary
wasn't about to let a *Time-Life* war correspondent die in
his territory, and he saw to it that I got the medicines I
needed, and even offered to fly me, if necessary, all the
way back to the U.S.A.

Would he have done the same for a sick American
newsman in Bucharest without the same connections?
Of course he would; but lying on my cot in the dim
bedroom, thinking in ever-widening circles about my
past, present and future, I couldn't see it that way at all.
The way I figured it, a man *had* to be part of some
organization just to exist; and I wasn't a part of anything
now. I must have been mad, I thought, to arrange things
like this. Just think! Nobody in any office anywhere was
waiting to hear from me, no secretary was making
travel arrangements to some fascinating place where a
blockbuster of a story awaited my attention; no editor
was chewing his nails waiting for me to phone in. Sometimes these thoughts hit me with such unbearable poi-
gnancy that tears came to my eyes and soaked freely
into the pillow in which I often buried my head, ostrich-
like, to shut out the world.

Withdrawal symptoms I call these thoughts now, and
sometimes we laugh about them. But at the time they
were very real. My mind would turn backward and go
over all the strange, odd, sometimes forlorn but always
fascinating places I had been to when I was a member
of the organization. Like the time I was stuck on a Greek
caïque in October 1944, proceeding to an unknown des-

tination with a skipper who was supposedly working for UNRRA, the United Nations Relief and Rehabilitation Administration, but whom I had discovered to be a black marketeer who was selling his supplies to starving people on islands in the Aegean Sea. I finally had to pull a gun on him, the first and only time I ever pulled a gun on anyone. It was an enormous .45 automatic cannon that had been thrust upon me by a British major who would not permit me to roam the Aegean Sea unarmed. Just in case my Greek skipper thought I was bluffing, I indulged occasionally in some target practice as we sailed onward, taking care to act as though I were used to shooting squirrels every morning for breakfast back home.

Or the time I nearly died from bacillary dysentery in Ankara. Turkey was even worse than Bucharest to be sick in because it was more an Oriental than a Western country, with customs that were completely alien to me. I lay in my bed for days, delirious with a roaring fever; only once did I manage to stagger out somewhere to see a Turkish doctor who was supposed to be able to help me. But I couldn't understand him and he couldn't understand me, and I came away with some huge yellow pills that seemed designed for horses rather than humans, and they did me no good at all.

I really thought I was going to die in Ankara—there didn't seem to be any way to stop me from dying. If the fever didn't get me, starvation would. Max Hill, a radio correspondent for NBC, and Pat Frank, who was then working for the Office of War Information, hovered over me anxiously every morning—they were my roommates in the big, old-fashioned Park Hotel. And one morning, in the dimness of a feverish stupor, I realized that a third person was bending over me: a small, slender man in the uniform of the U.S. Army Air Corps.

He was a doctor, and how Max and Pat found him I never learned. He had come in on a plane from Cairo, 23

the first American airplane, I was told, that the Turks—
then still neutral—allowed to land in Ankara. But they
did find him, and they told him that an American who
worked for *Time* and *Life* was dying in a hotel room,
and they brought him to me.

Later I was told that he spent two days and nights with
me, sitting by my bedside, watching to see if the sulfa
pills he miraculously had with him would save my life.
I don't even know his name.

That memory was good for a whole lot of weeping and
self-pity. The assumption on my part, of course, was
that he never would have come for just some free-lance
writer. "What's that?" I could hear him say to Pat and
Max. "Your roommate is dying of dysentery? Who's he?
Percy Knauth? Never heard of him. You'd better get him
to a doctor." And off he would fly back to Cairo, while my
life slowly ebbed away in the Park Hotel.

I chewed on ruminations like this endlessly, endlessly
in that shadowy room. As the days passed and the pain
gradually faded from my hip and thigh, I began to take
on a new identity: I became a person whose every
thought and move was plagued with doubts and fears.
I would wake up early in the morning and lie there
thinking: Jesus, where am I and how did I ever get here?
The fear would start its crawl up from my stomach
toward my brain, and when it reached my brain it paralyzed me. If I got up at all, I would limp around the
house like a zombie. The children, seeing me up, would
come to me with plans and projects as they always had;
I would snap at them, or give them a weak smile and,
feeling a hundred years old, spread out my hands in a
helpless gesture. I had one foot in the grave, but I
couldn't bear to tell them that. Our days of play and
work together were over, but I couldn't tell them that
either, so I would finally pull myself together and limp
to the beach with them, or go out in the boat; but I was
24   scared, scared, scared all the time.

When I could walk again, I got an office for myself. It was in a large, low building with a brick front on the other end of Water Street, and it was the best office anyone could have wished for. It was quiet; it had a window that looked out on a garden; it had a men's room just down the hall; it was paneled in wood, and it had bookshelves already in it. I installed my typewriter there, my typewriter paper, my books, my big Webster's Third, which I had brought back from France in my personal luggage. I hung some pictures on the walls, and bought a fan at Railroad Salvage, which blew cool September breezes in through the open window, bringing with them the scent of fading roses and yellowing grass. And one morning I sat down in that office with all the tools of my trade around me, everything I needed to be an Editor and a Writer, and tried to find my mind—the one essential tool which I seemed to have lost.

I can see that office now: cozy, snug, perfectly suited for my purposes—whatever the hell those were. There I signed the contract for a book about the North Woods that would appear—and ultimately did appear—in the Time-Life series on the American Wilderness, and I got a thousand dollars in exchange for just my signature. But nothing clicked in my mind, there was nothing that said: Boy! Here we go! I still had the whole damn book to write, didn't I?

I did a story for the Time-Life Nature/Science Annual there, too, and it earned me several thousand dollars. Furthermore, a researcher came all the way from New York to make some checking changes with me, and I told her to bring a bathing suit and we went down to the beach and talked about the article there, and swam. It was just as I used to imagine it would be in all those years when I dreamed of quitting the daily grind and becoming a free lance. But nothing clicked in my mind; nothing said: Well, boy, you're on your way! I was scared, scared, scared.

Every morning I would walk the half mile or so down Water Street, past the stores and shops of the village, and when I got to the office I would unlock the door of the building and call out a big "Hello, everybody! I'm here!" The place had just one drawback: the whole building was empty. There had been an oceanographic outfit there before, but they had gone bankrupt—oh, dreadful omen!—and I now occupied the building all by myself.

But even this didn't necessarily have to be a drawback. I would people the office with names and faces from what I was now piteously beginning to think of as the Good Old Days. Kay McCarthy would be sitting there, giving me a cheery smile as I walked past. Barbara Miller would lift her head from the dreary research she was doing and give me her usual short "Hi" without an exclamation point, and I would think, guiltily as always: I ought to have something better for her to do. (She *is* doing something better now; she got married and is raising horses with her husband in France.) Dick Johnston would be sitting at his desk, going over layouts for next week's issue of *Sports Illustrated.* And so on. And so forth.

It was a good try, and sometimes it worked—for a while. But then the figures would turn unsubstantial and fade away, and the silence would resume, and I would sit there, staring at my typewriter, thinking: What in hell *happened?* How did I ever get *here?*

Sometimes, in the golden September afternoons, my daughter, Lissie, would stop in to see me after school with her friend Sharon. Both were then about nine years old. Who needs ghosts for company when there are children like that around? There was a big, carpeted room right across the hall from mine, and with the yellow sunlight streaming in through the windows, making dappled shadows on the floor from the leaves of the apple tree that twinkled outside, the two girls would do cartwheels and rehearse the complex cheers with which, a little later in the season, they would spur on the high school football team. Over and over they would do those cheers, grave as little ballerinas as they went through the routines—then, at the end, they'd leap high into the air, shouting wildly and doing their cartwheels down the carpeted floor. After a half hour or so I would shoo them out, perhaps giving them money for an ice cream down at Roland's store, and go back to my work.

And to my fears. My ever-present, ceaseless, relentless and unmerciful fears.

Somewhere along in this time, I found myself sitting once again in the doctor's office—the same one I had gone to about the pain in my hip and thigh. I didn't have any pains anymore—except for those indescribable ones chasing each other around in my head all day—and all he wanted to do was check my blood pressure, which he had felt was a little high and bore some watching. I leafed idly through a magazine, trying not to think about how much I wanted a cigarette (smoking was frowned on in his office) and circling on my usual unremitting round of thoughts about what I was doing, where I was going, how we would live when the appalling punishment I felt was imminent would finally hit me, and all the rest of it.

Lately these thoughts had been getting grimmer. I couldn't really say why, but they were. There wasn't any reason. Our furniture had arrived at last and we were comfortably installed at home, the kids were well, there was money in the bank, and in my pursuit of survival I wasn't doing too badly. And yet the fear would not go away. . . .

Outside, the autumn day was dark and depressing, with rain in the air and a chill wind blowing. The countryside was already assuming the bleakness of winter, and the atmosphere of the waiting room—the mothers with their anxieties, their sniffling children, their obvi- 27 ous cares—depressed me even more. When I was finally ushered into the doctor's presence, I felt myself enveloped in an opaque cloud of gloom. Fear, doubt and guilt chased each other in my mind, leaving me, as they did so often now, feeling like a zombie who walks and talks but does not know who or where he is.

The doctor was brisk and cheerful as I took my seat. "Well, Percy," he said, "how've you been?"

For a moment I stared at him in utter bewilderment. Who was he? Where was I? What was I doing here? Above all, who is this guy who wants to know how I've *been?*

I couldn't even begin to find words to tell him. I sat there and stared at him, and then I burst into tears.

It was the first time I had given any outward manifestation of what was going on inside me, and when the dam burst it was—well, it was like a dam bursting. I wept uncontrollably. I shook, I sobbed, and the scalding tears streamed down my face. I can remember thinking, in honest astonishment: Jesus! What's happening to me now? But I couldn't stop, not for anything or anybody. I didn't even *want* to stop. For the first time in weeks I felt some release from the agony that had been pursuing me so relentlessly. I was going to tell somebody else about it, however awkwardly and melodramatically; above all, I was in the presence of someone who had stated in plain language that he was interested in knowing how I was. *Somebody cared.* That was all I needed to know.

Finally, I got some semblance of control over myself. The doctor, who was at first dumbfounded by my unexpectedly dramatic response to his innocent question, managed to evoke bits and pieces of the story from me, with the help of smelling salts and an arm around my shoulders, which steadied me and brought me a measure of comfort—a thing I had long since ceased to believe could exist. He got up at last and walked over to his desk.

"Blood pressure, hell," he said. "You're a sick man."

"But what's the matter with me?" I cried back at him. "I can't figure all this out. Am I losing my mind?"

There. I had said it out loud. I had finally put my worst fear into plain language. Now the roof would fall in. There could be only one answer to that question. Already my mind raced ahead in anticipation: a quieting shot in the arm, a strait jacket maybe, a trip to the hospital, and then, in due course, the ride to Norwich, to the state hospital for the insane, that grim, brick-walled building whose facade was already familiar from occasional drives by.

His answer was a total surprise to me. "You're not losing your mind," he said. "You're *sick.* You're suffering from a clinical case of involuted depression and we've got to do something for it right away."

The rest of that day is hazy in my memory. The only thing that I could think of was: It's got a name—this thing that's been plaguing me has got a name and something can be done about it. I know he gave me some pills that he said would help me until I got some real help. I know he took me out the door and watched me worriedly as I drove away; he had wanted to call my wife, but I had persuaded him that I could drive home safely. I know I did get home, and rushed distractedly through the house to the telephone, because he had also given me the name of a man I could call upon for expert consultation—a psychiatrist in a nearby town. I wanted nothing more than to see that man right away, *now,* and I could scarcely contain myself as I dialed the number. It rang, and rang, and rang; I didn't know whether I would break down again or scream.

The phone was picked up at last, but the nurse at the other end told me the doctor was busy with a patient. Did I want an appointment? Yes, I said, I urgently needed one. When could I come? I could be there in a half hour. . . .

"That won't be necessary," the cool voice said—and then came the crack of doom, matter-of-factly delivered over fifteen miles of telephone wire. "I can fit you in—let's see: yes—two weeks from today at four in the afternoon. Will that be satisfactory?"

Two weeks from today? Was the woman *mad*? Didn't she realize how close I was to the end of my tether? Didn't she *know* what a wait of two weeks meant to me?

I explained, as rationally as I could. I gave her the name of the doctor who was referring me. I said I was desperate. Perhaps psychiatric nurses become inured to the desperation in the voices that call them; perhaps they have to because there are so many of them. There was nothing I could do. Somehow I would have to survive for two weeks more.

It did not occur to me to call my own doctor back; he was an internist, and I felt he had done what he could. I clutched the pills that he had given me and tried to get used to the idea of waiting out a fortnight. The gray chill of autumn pressed in through the windows; a drizzle of rain began to fall. I was tired, unspeakably tired, but I knew that sleep would not come.

Two weeks more. I had to go on living like this two weeks more.

In the next two weeks I went through several more stages of my illness, and all of them led downward. They were, in order: bewilderment, resentment, rage and despair.

Identifying an illness usually has a double effect on a patient who is confused by what is happening to him.

Initially there is a feeling of relief: I now knew the name of what ailed me—although nothing of the nature or gravity of depression—and I knew that I was not alone. Others before me had been in the same situation, and others were in it now. Doctors knew about my illness, nurses had been trained to take care of patients like me. Medicines existed to alleviate my fears and miseries— eventually they might even effect a cure. I had—let's say —the mumps, the measles, the bubonic plague. Something could be done about me. All I had to do was wait.

This knowledge was of critical importance. I had been living too long in an isolated world. Ashamed of the fears that were pursuing me, I had not even told my wife how I was feeling. So I was all alone. I acted out a part before my family and occasionally wondered why nobody caught on, because my pretense seemed so false to me.

In the morning, after stumbling out of bed bleary-eyed from sleeplessness, I walked my troubles down Water Street to my office, there to wrestle with them all day long. Sometimes I succeeded in working for a while, burying myself in layouts and galleys. I had to produce twenty books in seven months. I had to assign writers to polish texts translated from a foreign language, I had to select pictures and plan page layouts, I had to find experts to check the finished products. It was a huge job, one that was almost impossible, as it would later develop; but I was too scared to think of that. The consequences of not getting my work done were so unmentionably awful that I could not face them.

But all the time, my bewilderment grew and grew and grew.

What *was* a "clinical case of involuted depression"? How did it happen to a man? Why? What had I done?

I had not the remotest idea. All I knew for certain in my errant mind was that I had been forsaken by the human race. God or divine Providence or whatever it might be that regulated human affairs had smitten me with a dreadful punishment in penance for some sin that I searched for endlessly and never found.

The nights were the worst. I started drinking more than usual, and often when I got to bed I was sodden with alcohol. I longed for sleeping pills, and rummaged everywhere to find some that might have been left over from my Paris days, when they were easier to come by. But pill or no pill, I never slept for more than three or four hours. Then I would awaken and lie there staring into the darkness while my mind began its endless circling again.

Thus I entered into the next phase of my illness: resentment of whatever it was that was wrong with me, and of whoever or whatever had visited this upon me.

I had to find a *reason*. For the first time that nightly cycle of thinking that went round and round between the twin poles of guilt and fear acquired a focal point. *Why* had this hit me? In the days and nights that dropped with agonizing slowness from the calendar I kept for D Day—Doctor Day—my endless questioning began to acquire a certain petulance. Waking at two or three o'clock, staring out into the night, I would dig deeper and deeper into my mind, testing this, rejecting that, never coming any closer.

Why, *why*, WHY? By slow degrees, petulance grew into active resentment: What the hell had I *done* to deserve this? Had I discovered that I had syphilis or gonorrhea, I could at least point to some illicit intercourse as the reason; but goddamnit, this was *senseless!* And with the resentment, there came gradually a note of violence and rage, and the swear words, great, black globs of unspeakable obscenities, would rage into my thoughts until, lying in bed beside my wife, I would literally shake with fury.

Next came despair. It was as black as all the legions of darkness I had ever heard about, and it came at me screaming.

This was the first really desperate time in those two 33

weeks of waiting. When I look back on those times now, I understand why doctors fear depression. I was sometimes literally mad with rage. I think that—thank God —my wife sensed this. I might have killed her in the most trivial argument and I am surprised that with all that towering fury inside of me, I did not kill myself.

I was not arguing with myself about death at this time; I was not really thinking about it. If I had killed myself, it would have been a mad, impulsive accident, a twist of the wheel when I was driving down the highway. But some part of me stayed careful about driving in that time. I knew my rage enough to make it part of my ever-present fear.

The doctor's pills did nothing at all, except to plague me with their name. They were small and blue, and I could never get the name straight. I worried about it all night long: "Etrafon" or "Etranof"—it was like one of those made-up science fiction names and it got all mixed up in my mind. Whatever they were called, they brought me no relief and when I ran out of them one day I did not even bother to call the doctor to get more.

My work was slowly turning into a nightmare, too. In the beginning, I had planned to go to New York perhaps once a month for editorial conferences; now I had to go at least once a week to try to get the translations and the pictures that I needed. Somebody had goofed; it finally came out that there were no translations yet, so to the long list of my concerns I now had to add the worry of where to find an agency that could translate close to a million words by the day before yesterday. Even the trains conspired against me. One gloomy Sunday night I rode to New York on a train that consisted of a single ancient passenger car hooked to a Penn Central locomotive. The seats were broken, the windows filthy, the floor littered with debris. I thought it fitting transportation for a man who had sunk as low as I.

34   D Day came at last. When that last page dropped from

the calendar I was keeping, I was worn out. I had no fight left, no more strength for anger. I could struggle only feebly with my work. To my wife I was a shadow, and she was worried.

She knew that I was going to see a psychiatrist, but she did not really know why. I still had not told her of the awful things that were happening in my head. How could I? If they frightened me, would they not terrify her? The doctor would take care of that somehow. He had to. He was the only hope I had left.

By now I had experienced all the classic symptoms of depression, one after another. As the lack of sleep wore me down, a sense of hopelessness enveloped me. I knew that nothing I did could change this situation. There was nothing I *could* do. I was convinced that I was laboring under some kind of curse so that any efforts of my own to fight this situation were foredoomed to failure.

More realistically, I understood that the only tool I could fight with—my mind—was the very part of me that was affected. Can a legless man get up and walk even if he knows that only walking will save his life? My mind was going; how could I use it to extricate myself from my despair?

With this hopelessness came the final stage in my loss of self-esteem: in my own eyes I became worthless. In long night sessions, I reviewed my life and saw everything that I had done wrong. Not even the most trivial detail escaped this deadly scrutiny. I remembered arguments I had had with my older children when they were very young, in my first marriage, and I realized what a poor excuse for a father I had been. I recalled the details of my divorce, and I understood precisely why my first wife had left me for another man: I had never really filled the role of husband. Viewed in the merciless gloom of this early-morning self-analysis, even my work appeared to me to have been a fraud. At last I was 35 being showed up for the hapless faker that I was, and this was my punishment.

Such notions are not sane, but how could I know this? They seemed terribly plausible. Whenever I tried to tell myself that I was being irrational, I came up against that other, even more unthinkable, truth: that I was going crazy. And since this was undeniably so . . . But I shrank from that and tried to think of the psychiatrist whom I would shortly see. One way or another, I would get the truth from him.

I drove off to his office on a chilly November day. The long black branches of the trees reached hopelessly up into an unforgiving sky. Dead, wet leaves glistened in the gutters as I drove by, and the black streets gleamed in a drizzling rain. It matched the chill in my soul.

The doctor's house was small and gray beneath towering trees. A sad-faced nurse ushered me silently into a gloomy reception room. A few old magazines lay on a table; I picked one up. It was *Sports Illustrated,* which I had helped to launch sixteen years before and on which I had been text editor for eight years. I could not bear to be reminded of those happy times so long ago, and put it down again. I waited, alone as usual with my thoughts.

Twenty minutes later I was sitting in a brown leather armchair beside the doctor's desk, in a dim room with drawn curtains. A single lamp shone on the desk, and the doctor's face was in shadow. The room was very quiet. He waited for me to speak.

I tried to tell him of my fears, my awful nights, my endless rounds of questioning, my rage, my hopelessness, my feelings that at fifty-seven, after a worthless, misspent life, I had reached the limit of anything I could do. My words seemed inadequate. Those two weeks I had waited—those terrible two weeks of agony! I could not even begin to describe them.

36   I did not break down and weep this time. I had no

tears left in me, no emotions strong enough to break the spell that paralyzed me.

His first words surprised me.

"Have you ever thought of suicide?"

It took me a long time to formulate an answer. I felt it was a desperately important question. Had I? Had I? Sometime long ago, I had read that the person who talks about committing suicide will never actually do it. Did this apply as well to *thinking* about suicide? What was the right answer, the one that would make the strongest impression on this quiet man who represented my last hope?

"Yes," I said at last. "I guess I have."

He asked me how I had thought about it, under what circumstances. Had I planned how I would do it?

I was still uncertain. I wanted terribly to get through to him, to make him realize how urgently I needed help. Was this the right way to go about it?

I could not truthfully say that I had ever planned my own death. I told him lamely about those fleeting impulses I occasionally had when driving—a sudden twist of the wheel, a plunge through the rail of the New London bridge, or a head-on crash. . . .

He did not seem impressed. He went through other questions in a formal way—where had I grown up, what did I think about my childhood, was I happily married? I answered in a formal way. I had the feeling that I had flunked the first question, and therewith the examination.

I also sensed, in a despairing way, that the doctor was leading me onto familiar territory. Déjà vu. I had been here before.

Almost twenty years earlier, in an effort to save my first marriage, I had gone twice a week for six months to a psychiatrist in Berlin. Those were intensive sessions, and I later realized that they had changed my life in some important ways. The doctor there had been a

Jungian, a middle-aged man with frizzly white hair and a deep, almost mystic way of thinking about the world, the universe, and the universal unconscious that links all mankind. He had communicated these things to me in hours of talk that probed so deeply into my secret being that when I left him and walked home down the wintry Berlin streets, I sometimes felt that I had been turned inside out and was looking at myself from some vantage point high above me, seeing myself as the small, striving creature that I was. I liked myself much better when I was through with him, and if these sessions did not save my marriage, they certainly made me a stronger, more self-reliant person than I had been before.

Or so I had thought. The way I felt now was altogether different from the way I had felt then. At that time, I was trying to understand myself, and even more to understand my wife, whom I deeply loved and who had suddenly found so many deficiencies in me that she wanted to leave me. But now, some twenty years later and thousands of miles from Berlin, I did not need understanding; I needed rescue. All my words, which seemed so lame to me, could have been summarized in a single, desperate cry: *Help!*

But where was I going now? Where was all this leading me? There seemed no point in treading again those paths I had followed in Berlin; I had explored them thoroughly. Surely there had to be a different way of treating the illness that was afflicting me now. . . .

But when I left, I was not sure. The doctor had told me a few things about depression. It might go on for six months more, or for two more years. What we could do together would depend on what we found together, inside me. It was far too early to say now. Meanwhile, here were some antidepressant pills that I should take three times a day.

38 When I reached home, my wife questioned me ea-

gerly, and for the first time I was able to recognize the depth of her concern. It touched me, and I tried to tell her what hope I had derived from this session, for which she knew I had been waiting so long. But my words stumbled over each other; I did not know what to say. I didn't have much hope, if truth were told, but I did not want to tell her that. I didn't want to drag her down with me. I certainly didn't want her to know that all my days and nights were spent in fear.

And I didn't want to tell her that what I actually saw before me was a long and devious and probably unrewarding journey far back into my past.

My visits to the doctor slowly settled into a routine. His office was half an hour's drive from my home and at first, despite my initial misgivings, I looked forward to each visit with some anticipation—there was relief in simply talking to someone. Then I noticed a change in my feelings toward him. It began to dawn on me that I didn't really have anyone to talk *to;* he was only somebody to talk *at.* No matter what I said, I scarcely ever got what I would consider to be an enlightening reply. Whenever I paused in my monologue, waiting for an answer from him, he usually said only, "Please go on."

He was an extraordinary listener, so quiet, so unobtrusive that he could easily have traded places with his own shadow. He performed perfectly the role that Sigmund Freud long ago defined for the psychoanalyst: emotional catalyst and sounding board. But I didn't need psychoanalysis. I could hear my own self talking as we sat in the dimness of his consultation room, and my words were strange and foreign to my ears, as if completely unrelated to my problem.

Each of us was searching for a different thing. He thought of my depression as a neurosis, the deep-seated roots of which he wanted to expose and sever. All I wanted was release from this prison in which I was slowly going to pieces. I didn't have the wit or nerve to 39 tell him this outright; who was I to criticize his treatment? Most of all I feared losing control, and I spent most of my days and nights trying desperately to keep myself together. If I ever did let go, I was afraid I would fall apart completely and have to be hospitalized. He never prodded me toward that brink; what might have happened if he had? We simply plodded backward through my life in an exercise that I found increasingly frustrating.

Invariably I spent the half hour drive to his office thinking of what I would—or could—say to him that day. This wasn't easy, because I had long since run out of things to talk about with a psychoanalyst. By the mid-1950s, after my divorce, I had become something of a veteran of the couch. Since Berlin, I had sought aid and counsel several times. I had consulted with Freudians and Jungians, I had probed my psyche in three languages—my God, I knew the drill! Dreams, free associations, random thoughts that appear repetitively like a knocking on the door—these were the things an analyst looked for. So I always tried to come up with something promising that could be spun out into a meaningful fifty-minute monologue under the doctor's wise old eyes.

But I couldn't remember my dreams anymore; I felt I hadn't dreamed for months. Now all my dreams were *real.* I couldn't allow myself any free associations; they led me instantly into a downward spiral so dizzy and frightful that I had to close my eyes and hang on to something to keep a measure of control. And my repetitive thoughts were nonsense, like "Etrafon."

And anyway, those weren't wise old eyes looking at me as I rambled on through visit after visit. The few times that I saw them they looked tired and withdrawn and they were younger eyes than mine. I was probably the doctor's senior by ten years.

40   Yet in all those sessions with him I tried, *really* tried,

to tell him what was happening to me. I tried to recapture for his benefit the blackness of night, the utter silence, the lonely wail of the foghorn drifting over from Watch Hill Light, the desolation of being lost in space with no light to steer by, no possibility of ever coming to rest. I never felt that I succeeded. And I always had this queer sense of detachment, as though I were talking about somebody else. He listened quietly to it all, sometimes tapping his teeth reflectively with a pencil, sometimes scribbling a few notes, often gazing out into space past my own pleading eyes, as though his mind were on something far away.

A new thought came to me: Was I wasting his time? This only increased still further the burden of guilt under which I labored. But since *I* was paying *him* to help *me,* I could see even in my distress that this was completely unreasonable and I found myself growing irritated, then angry. What the hell was the matter with me anyway? Here was a guy being *paid* to listen to me and I couldn't even get a dialogue going. I just seemed to bore him.

In this halting, stumbling fashion we explored my childhood, which grew increasingly uninteresting as we struggled backward through the years. I had long ago concluded that it was a pretty good childhood, all in all; the usual hang-ups now and then, of course, the confusions and pains that go with growing up, but nothing that might interest a psychoanalyst. Once there was a brief flash of promise: I hit on a childhood dream, just remembered, that looked as though it might be developed into something of sexual significance. It had happened *very* long ago, and it had to do with a sister who crept into my room one night and tried to strangle me —in the dream, that is. But that trail quickly petered out. I couldn't find any trace of sex in it, and the dream had nothing whatever to do with any of my sisters.

What we did get into, for a while, was the peculiar 41

(but well known to me) anomaly that I literally never knew anything factual about sex until I was about fifteen years old, when I began to pick up the steamy details from other kids at school. But this was barren ground that I had trod before. What it added up to was simply that these things were never talked about in my family—which was pretty much the rule in those days —and that I did not even know a penis was called a penis, much less what it was used for in adult life. I didn't know anything about menstruation either, despite the fact that I grew up with three sisters. I went right up to my twenties with some odd, distorted notions about sex. I thought that all women disliked it and endured it only because they had to, and that there was something of the beast in any man's sexual desires, including of course my own. Also, someone way back when had told me that the best way to get rid of them was not to look for a girl who was willing but to find a good, hard board and lie down flat on my back for a while, or take a cold shower, or better still, find a lake and take a flying leap into it.

In short, I had learned long since that there was nothing fundamentally traumatic in all this for me, only a profound, regrettable and rather ridiculous ignorance that hadn't really done me any harm.

There was one other childhood thing, but I didn't need an analyst to tell me what significance it had. When I was fourteen, my parents decided it was time for me to go forth into the world and learn about life in a good prep school. The one my father had gone to when he was fourteen was an obvious choice in a tradition-minded family, so off I went one fine September day. I had a couple of weeks of terrible homesickness, but then I discovered an unsuspected aptitude for football: I could run like a rabbit with the ball. I became a sort of star on the third team, which did my ego a world of good and relieved me of anxieties about my future in a masculine world: I could always make it as a football player.

But then came Thanksgiving, and a visit from my parents. It was the first time I had seen them in nearly three months, and though I spent a happy day showing them around and performed nobly for them on the gridiron, the whole thing came apart when it was time for them to go. My homesickness rose like a volcano inside me, I burst into a torrent of tears, my mother was horrified, my father confused—and it ended with them taking me back home that same evening and returning me to the day school where I had been before.

Years later, an analyst tried to interpret the whole thing as a symbolic castration, but this never made sense to me. For one thing, I did fine at the day school, and in the big game of the baseball season against our archrival, I stepped up to the plate in the ninth inning with two out and whacked a bases-loaded homer that won the game and sent all the girls right out of their minds. This just didn't seem like the act of a boy who had been made a spiritual eunuch.

But that it was a personal defeat of sorts I recognized very well, at the time, and I never forgot the lesson. There wasn't any psychological significance left in it for me, though, and I couldn't stretch it over more than two sessions this time, either.

There remained my first marriage. That should be a mother lode of psychological drama—enough, I thought, to set Freud to twittering in his grave. It was a story that had begun in Berlin some thirty-one years before, in the pre-Pearl Harbor times of World War II when I was working in the Nazi capital for the New York *Times*. It had come to its shocking end thirteen years later, in 1953, a year that really did convulse my life. But while I was right in anticipating that I might find the taproot of my depression buried in here some-where, I was wrong in thinking that it lay in my divorce. 43

Ultimately, I was to find out that it was not the end at all, but the beginning that traumatized me—but that realization did not come in a doctor's office.

I had never recapitulated the Berlin beginnings of this marriage for any previous therapist, and I did not do so now. It was a bitter-lovely memory, which I buried deliberately after my first wife divorced me. The divorce was a mind-cracking blow to me, so painful that I never let myself retrace the Berlin years again. It was over, and I wanted to forget it for good.

As for the divorce itself, when I brought it back now in that dim office under the doctor's noncommittal eye, I found nothing in it but expected and remembered pain. I remembered everything with extraordinary clarity, and I made the most of it.

I was able to recall every detail and every sickening emotion felt on my arrival home in 1951 from seven months in Europe, when I landed at La Guardia Airport —Idlewild, now JFK, wasn't finished yet—and there was no wife to meet me at the plane. That was when the whole divorce thing started. Lugging suitcases, I ran for half an hour from one phone booth to another, dropping nickels in every one of them without ever getting a dial tone. I thought the world had gone mad—why were *all* the telephones at La Guardia out of order? A kindly passer-by finally explained: while I was off in Europe the rate had been doubled to ten cents.

It was like that all the way through, with an edge of black comedy. It wasn't *real* to me anymore; the years since it had happened had done their healing work. The divorce had been extremely painful, yes; but I was certainly not mortally wounded. When it was over and my ex-wife had departed for Paris with her new husband and our four sons, I had gone on a wild sex spree with several girls I knew, but after a while I settled down, got a job and finally remarried, this time to a woman who 44 seemed to have none of the wandering predilections and strange, unsatisfied desires of the dear departed whom I had loved for so long. My second wife and I even succeeded, after three miscarriages and a stillborn child, in building a family of our own to replace the four boys I had lost—and this family included the daughter I had always longed for. And in their adolescence, as the years went by, my older boys sometimes came to live with me, thus closing the circle and making it possible for me to make up for some of the years I had missed between.

All in all, 1953 had settled down in my mind as a memorably difficult year, but there wasn't anything truly traumatic about it—not anymore.

And so it went. I traveled the long road through my life with my analyst for seven months, and I might be traveling it still, sitting there for fifty minutes every week talking to a man who sometimes didn't seem to be there at all. Fifty minutes—and then my time was up. "I'm sorry," he would say apologetically. "We will have to stop now; I have another patient waiting." And I would say good-by and climb wearily into my car and drive back to my village, no wiser than before—only sadder.

It might still be going on—I have known these analyses to last for years, while both parties grow old and gray and become as familiar to each other as man and wife—but for the fact that the twenty-book series I was responsible for in my work was beginning to get the better of me. In January, I realized that if ever I was going to get this job done I would have to have an office in New York and someone to help me. An office was provided in a fancy new building on Third Avenue, and an energetic angel who wore ravishing woolen pants suits was taken off the reception desk and sent to me. She proved to be a compulsive organizer, just what I needed. I, who a few short months before had felt so deprived of all friends and associates in my empty office 45 on Water Street, was beginning to build a staff of my own and wasn't even aware of it.

At the same time, the daily and nightly fights with fear went on. I saw the doctor once a week on Monday mornings, before driving back to New York after a weekend at home. The locale for my terrors now shifted to the little attic room, where I was really all alone. My struggle entered what almost proved to be its final, fatal phase.

6

I began my dialogue with death on a bleak March morning some two months after I had moved to the New York office and my attic room.

It was cold; the earth was frozen iron hard beneath an iron sky. I was walking to work through New York's Central Park in the half light of early morning. A light snow was falling.

I crossed the road that winds northward past granite outcroppings to the Seventy-second Street transverse. The park seemed deserted; nothing stirred. Then, ahead of me through the trees, I saw the steadily blinking light of a police car pulsing through the gloom.

In spring the children's playground here is alive with cries and movement. Now the swings were still, and snow slithered silently down the empty slides. Near the entrance to the playground, alone on the hard earth beneath a tree that spread skeletal branches skyward, lay a dead man.

He was middle-aged, perhaps a couple of years older than I. He was dressed in a worn black coat partially buttoned over a torn heavy brown sweater. His cracked brown shoes had newspapers stuffed into them in place of socks. He lay on his back, arms outflung as though in resignation. He had a round bald head and a broad Slavic face, and in that face his faded blue eyes were wide open and staring at the sky.

Snow fell on those open eyes and lay there, giving them a misty sheen.

The police car was parked a few yards away. Two patrolmen sat in it, smoking and talking in low tones. Above their heads, the blinking light turned slowly round and round and round.

I stared at the body. The trousers had slid up on his legs, and on his shins the thin pink flesh was beginning to turn gray. There was no mark of violence on him; he was at peace. Whatever might have happened to him, it was over now.

He looked like a man who had done much traveling, perhaps sixty years' worth, through some very distant places. There was something vaguely familiar about him, but I couldn't decide what it was. Could I have seen him before?

I stood there for a long time, staring down at him, and gradually it came to me. I *had* seen him before, countless times and in countless places—him, and dozens like him. I had seen him wandering the roads of eastern Germany in 1939, in that golden September when the blitzkrieg destroyed Poland. I had seen him in the railroad station of Istanbul in 1944, desperately trying to elude the Turkish police who were sending him and hundreds of other Jews back to Germany with forged passports supplied by the German embassy. I had seen him in the concentration camp of Buchenwald when it was liberated in the spring of 1945; he was a starving skeleton then, mobbing me with his frenzied fellow prisoners when I unwisely started offering them chocolate. I had seen him trudging eastward that same spring, in his tattered blue-and-white-striped concentration camp uniform, wearing with pride the emblems of a racial prisoner, the letters *KL*—for *Konzentrationslager*—and the yellow star of Jewry. I had seen him plodding westward, home toward France or Holland, on the dusty roads of Germany's defeat.

He was a refugee.

What had happened to this man? I had no way of knowing. He lay there, thousands of miles from wherever his home might have been before the merciless war snatched him up and threw him away, dead on the frozen ground in the lightly falling snow. I wished that I could close his eyes.

The image of his dead face stayed with me. It fitted uncannily into my own darkening mood. I could not shake the memory of his empty, staring eyes filmed over by the falling snow. I could sometimes lose it in the daytime when I was caught up in the crises of work to be done in the office, but at night I was haunted.

And one night, seeing that face again, I realized why. His was not the face of a man who had been punished by death. On the contrary, he had had about him the aura of one who had found in death some sort of Holy Grail.

49

From that moment on I identified my own internal struggle with him. My yearning for a respite became a yearning for the peace that he had found. I felt that he had been a wanderer like me whose quest was over now. Mine went on.

If I joined him, might I find my answer, too?

This was the night that marked the beginning of my deadly argument with the dark power of suicide. It was a terribly unequal struggle, and there were times when I was more than ready to give in. Death seemed to hold all the cards of logic and persuasion; I had nothing on my side beyond the fact that I was still alive. I did not really want to die. And yet . . .

"What is the point of this struggle?" the image of the dead man seemed to say to me. "A man grows older, and wiser, and finally there comes a time when all his wisdom clearly shows him that there *is* no point to it: what he is doing is merely obeying an instinct to stay alive. A little longer, or perhaps a lot longer—what does it matter in the end? Death will always win."

"Look at me here now," he seemed to say another night. "I lie on my back in a strange city, a whole lifetime away from the place where I was born. What has happened to everything I dreamed of accomplishing when I was a boy? What does it matter now what I did succeed in doing? Had I been president of Poland, or dictator of all the Russians, or premier of France—I would still have ended up lying dead somewhere, perhaps with snow falling on my open eyes. But the snow is warm and nothing matters anymore. I have found peace."

Peace! The word whispered in the shadows of my quiet room. I had only to reach out and it could be mine.

Feebly I fought back the temptation, but I was losing heart. It grew more and more difficult for me to argue. I was very tired, and my mind was increasingly prone to those sudden, terrible sideways slips that blacked me out for an instant—an instant only, but an instant of eternity. I was losing my faith that the future held any promise of relief from my nightmare. And I always came up against the same unanswerable question: What was I struggling *for?*

Round and round that question went while I argued with the image of the dead man. Back through the well-worn trail of my whole life I argued with him, finding little that might help me.

There had been a time, long years before, when I had struggled very hard against great odds for something I believed in passionately: a love and a marriage and a child. That was in Berlin, when I was very young and World War II had just begun. But why go back to that? That was the chapter I had cut out of my life after my divorce. That was all dead and gone; it meant nothing to me anymore. That had been a young man's fancy, and I was past my middle fifties now. . . .

So when it surged, I put that memory aside, and then there came at last to my mind another time and another face—a time when I was living in Sag Harbor, the old whaling village far out toward the tip of Long Island, in the final months before my first marriage ended in 1953.

I had a great and good friend in Sag Harbor, the Polish poet Kasimir Wierzynski. He was perhaps twenty years older than I, and when I first knew him he had been living the life of a refuge and an exile for more than a decade. I have never known a man in whom the spark of life burned more ebulliently. He was a poet in the most beautiful sense of the word: he saw life from the inside outward, and no matter what life did to him, he thought that simply being alive was a marvelous gift of God.

Kasimir and I were partners in poverty in those days; we had no money at all. I had quit my job with *Life* to try and save my marriage, and I made what I could by selling an occasional story. I don't know what he lived on, but I know that of the two of us, he was the richer because he had faith. We had a little joke we used to share.

Every morning after breakfast, we would meet and walk together down to the post office to pick up our mail. And as we met, he would say to me:

"Percy! Good morning, my dear friend! Do you know what is going to happen today?" And he would look at me expectantly with his strong, laughing eyes.

"Today? Why should today be any different?"

"Because ... I will tell you why. Because today we will each of us find in our mailbox a check for fifty thousand dollars!"

I would feign amazement. "Fifty thousand dollars! Who is going to send me fifty thousand dollars, Kasimir?"

"Ah, my friend! You do not know this yet, but this is what you will get for writing the Great American Novel! As for me, I have just finished a poem so beautiful that it will make the angels weep. You must never forget that we are Writers of Importance, my friend! I am a poet, and you—you have worked for the great magazines like *Time* and *Life* that can make the world stand still! And do you know what we will do when we have found these checks?"

"Carry on, Kasimir!"

"We will bring them to the bank and there we will ask to see the president. When he comes out to us, we will give the checks to him and say, 'Here! Deposit these!' This will instantly make of us Very Big Men. And then we will draw out a huge sum of money, and we will gather up our wives, and we will take your car and go to the best restaurant on Long Island and have a stupendous meal. We will order bottles of slivovitz and we will get very, very drunk. And when we wake up from our drunkenness the next morning—*tomorrow* morning, my dear friend—the whole world will be different!" And he would burst into a roar of laughter and clap me on the back, and we would walk on, and no matter what the weather was that morning or what was on my mind, the world would be different already.

It was a foolish, joyous little joke. There never was a check for fifty thousand dollars and we never succeeded in changing the world. My wife divorced me and I moved back to New York alone to find a job. A year or so after that, Kasimir and his wife left Sag Harbor and went back to Europe to live precariously in Paris, London and wherever else he could find shelter for a time. He never stopped writing the poetry that so few people could read in its original language—he was not published in his native Poland—and he never stopped believing in the marvelous gift of life. When he was struck down by a heart attack in March 1969, the memory of his presence in the world shone like a blessing in the London church that was crowded with his friends and admirers. I wept at his graveside, thinking of the foolish and wonderfully defiant gaiety we had shared all those years before.

I lay in my attic room after my futile arguments with the dead man in the park, wishing that Kasimir were alive to help me now. But such was my distracted state of mind that knowing he was dead was only an added inducement to cross over to the other side and join him. I did not realize until long afterward how my old friend was helping me even then, just through my memory of him. The life of Kasimir Wierzynski, poet, was the most powerful answer I could possibly have found to the nightly blandishments of death.

Sometime in April, my arguments with the dead man in the park ended in my surrender. On that rainy dawn in the little attic room I gave up. The coming night, I decided, I would kill myself. I had had enough. Inside my head the clamorous voices were stilled at last. The face of the dead man in the park faded away forever. 53

Of course, I did not do it; my wife pulled me back from the brink and refused to let me go. But that *was* the morning I hit bottom.

I did not go to work that day; I was physically incapable of doing so. I sat in a chair with a tray on my knees while my wife fed me breakfast. My arms and legs shook uncontrollably, my knees clattered. The world was a blur. My mind slipped and slid. I could not hold on to it; it was as transparent, as unsubstantial and as slippery as a jellyfish. If my wife had not spent the night in town and been there that morning, I am certain that I would eventually have stumbled out onto the roof, sat on its edge and let myself go. It needed just a word from somewhere.

But the dead man in the park was gone. It was my wife who gave me the word. "Eat," she said, and I ate.

That evening, after a very quiet, gentle day, a startling fact came home to me. I had missed a day at work, an entire day. Tomorrow I would surely miss another. But the world had not collapsed. None of my children had died of hunger. My job had not dissolved in chaos. On the contrary, my office staff was unconcerned, knowing I would be back in a day or two. "Tell him to take it easy," my associate editor told my wife when she phoned in to report me sick. "Everything is going fine here."

I hit bottom—and I touched reality. At last I had something under my feet again. I had a long way to go, but that was the evening I started my slow way up again. Somewhere in my mind the fact had registered that all those wild turmoils of which I had been so helpless a victim were not founded on anything real. It was a very small thing, quite tentative, but it was enough for a new beginning.

The spring wore on. The job neared its end. The twenty books I was preparing slowly piled up on my
desk: words, pictures, page layouts neatly arranged and

ready for the printer. I never really noticed until the final weeks that I had built an organization where nothing had existed before. I had an office staffed with my own people, and these people had worked well.

There came a day when the books were done and I was able to go home again.

7

When I returned to Connecticut in the early summer of 1971, I began a new life. This was the life I had dreamed of so often in the past, with a little office on the top floor of my home (the cozy office down on Water Street had disappeared, melted indistinguishably into a complex of apartments created in the building) and unlimited time to pursue the books and magazine articles I had in mind. It should have been the beginning of a happier time. But the fears remained.

They were as bad as ever. They woke me to predawn blackness each morning, they dogged my every act by day, they haunted me each evening before I fell into uneasy, restless sleep. Only one thing had changed. I no longer thought of suicide. I had ended my dialogue with death, and though I had finally surrendered, miraculously I had survived. Now there was the grimmer prospect of continuing to live.

It was sometime during that period that I remembered an incident of a few months before, a morning in March when my wife had chanced on an article in the New York *Times.* "When the Diagnosis Is Depression," ran the headline, and the story told of a group of psychiatric researchers under the direction of one Dr. Eugene S. Paykel who were studying depression in cooperation with the Connecticut Mental Health Center and the Yale University Department of Psychiatry in New Haven, only sixty miles away from my home.

The article had briefly excited my interest and aroused my hopes, but both had faded when I learned that my psychiatrist had never heard of the Depression Research Unit, or of its director, Dr. Paykel. I had stuck the clipping into a desk drawer where I kept all sorts of letters, newspaper clippings and magazine articles that might someday develop into stories or a book. Now I searched the drawer, found the clipping, read it—and an idea blossomed. If I was going to have to go on suffering this way for an indefinite period of time, I might as well turn it to my account. I would do a magazine article on depression and see if I could sell it to my old friends at *Life* magazine.

I thought about it for a day, and it felt right. Even if nothing developed in the way of a magazine piece, I would certainly learn something more about the illness 57 that had been eating away at me for so long. The next morning I called up the Depression Research Unit and got an appointment to go and see them.

Why hadn't I applied for treatment there months ago? For one thing, there was my own psychiatrist's lack of knowledge about the place, a discouraging indication that probably the people in New Haven had nothing to offer that might help me. There was also the fact that I was afraid. There was no assurance that the New Haven people would take me on as a patient; I lived far beyond the area they supposedly covered, and had they refused me, I was not sure my fragile hopes of recovery could survive.

The idea for a magazine article solved all that. I didn't even have to tell them I was depressed. I could ask questions and listen and learn, and maybe I could even learn something with which I could help myself. So, one bright day in early July, I was on Interstate 95 heading toward New Haven.

When I arrived at the address given to me over the telephone, my first reaction was an intense stab of disappointment.

I faced a shabby old brick tenement on a side street, less than a block away from some of the bright new buildings put up in the years of New Haven's drive for urban renewal. It looked like a place that had accidentally survived the demolition program. The bricks were soot-stained and ancient, the windows drear. A few paper notices were pinned to the door. "Ring and walk in" —that sort of thing—and a faded sign identified the building as part of the Psychiatric Division of the Yale–New Haven Medical Center.

Inside, two girls were typing busily at a couple of desks in a reception room off a gloomy hallway. Two armchairs that looked as though they had been purchased from a Salvation Army warehouse stood in a bay window on which faded yellow shades were half pulled down. On a battered table lay some old magazines. A poster of Andrew Wyeth's painting *Christina's World* was tacked up on one wall. Poor Christina! That old house on the hill toward which she looked with such intense longing seemed as shabby as my hopes of finding my salvation—here or anywhere else.

One of the girls stopped typing for a minute and looked up at me.

"Can I help you?"

"Yes," I said, and identified myself. "I'm here to see Dr. Myrna Weissman."

Dr. Weissman is an epidemiologist, and I had spoken to her on the phone the week before. Today she is the director of the place, and I have seen her many times and never failed to be warmed by her radiance. But on that morning I expected—I don't know what. A dried-up, bureaucratic welfare type, perhaps, or somebody with steel glasses and the mind of a computer programmer. Certainly not this woman in an attractive short skirt and gaily printed blouse who came down the stairs and cordially shook my hand.

She was young—somewhere in her mid-thirties, I would guess—she was petite, and her smile lit up her whole face and crinkled her eyes appealingly. She led me up a flight of threadbare carpeted steps and into a little office whose single window looked out on an alley full of weeds and cinders. There was another of the leftover-looking desks in it, a couple of chairs, some filing cabinets, and that was all.

"Well," she said, sitting down behind the desk and smiling brightly. "What can I do for you?"

I explained. I told her about the article in the *Times,* which she remembered. I told her this had aroused my interest in depression and that I wanted to learn as much as I could about it. I said it was an illness that seemed worth writing about because it appeared to be widespread and yet so little known.

She agreed about its being widespread. "Oh, yes, indeed," she said. "It is much more common than most people realize. Depression is a human phenomenon that can hit anyone. It ranges from adolescence to old age, and it can be a very serious thing. If anyone thinks he is suffering from it, he should see his doctor in the same way that he would go to him for any other illness."

I must have talked to her for more than an hour, filling pages in my notebook with the things she told me. There were still considerable differences of opinion about the diagnoses of depression, she said, particularly between British and American doctors, who seemed to be the leaders of an investigative effort that pretty well covered the world. The British were more likely to diagnose depression, while Americans often classified its symptoms as one of the milder forms of schizophrenia. This was the first time I realized that the line between depression and schizophrenia can be shadowy and difficult to draw, and that the relationship between the two is still a matter of considerable research and debate. "If you get a really severely depressed person," Dr. Weissman said, "it may be very hard to tell if he isn't schizophrenic. Once in a while you may even encounter depressed persons who have mild hallucinations."

Also often confused with depression is what more and more doctors are calling "bipolar" depression, more familiar to laymen as manic depression. This is a disease of violent cyclical mood swings, from "highs" of wild elation, dynamic energy and illusionary feelings of strength and capability to paralyzing "lows" of deep depression. There may be a genetically-rooted factor in bipolar depression, and it accounts for only about 5 percent of all mental illness. The incidence of unipolar depression, by contrast, is staggering—about ten in every hundred Americans can expect to suffer from depression at least once in their lifetime.

There are differences in degree in depressive illnesses, and also differences in kind; but although many efforts have been made over the years to sort these out, no reliable classification has as yet been achieved. The existence of too many areas of disagreement and the lack of enough accurate statistical data make it impossible to say: This and this and this are true of such and such a form of depression. But it is generally agreed that there are two basic types of depression, which is a little like saying, "There are two basic types of breakdown in an automobile engine—mechanical failures and ignition failures." In other words, it helps, but not much.

The two basic forms of depression are exogenous and endogenous, sometimes—and more simply—also called reactive and biologic depressions. This is to a certain degree misleading, however, since it implies that a depression is either one kind or the other. Actually, any depression has both a reactive and a biologic component; the difference lies in which component is dominant. As one scientific expert puts it: "They are not necessarily different conditions but different points on a spectrum of severity." Let us examine each kind more closely and see just what the difference is.

Reactive depressions involve, first of all, some incident (or life event, as doctors call it) that precipitates a reaction—the loss of a loved one, loss of a job, severe financial problems and the like. This may occur in combination with a history of previous neurotic traits and the kind of emotional vulnerability that reacts quickly, easily or excessively to disturbing factors in life.

Biologic depressions are generally diagnosed on the basis of symptoms that go deeper, are more lasting and, in the absence of an obvious precipitating life event, are less easily explained. Among other elements, they *may* involve delusions, a slowing down of muscular activity, a variation in severity of symptoms between morning and evening, and a family history of depression.

The distinction between reactive and biologic depressions is often confusing and can lead to problems in making a diagnosis. For example, the severity of a depression after a precipitating life event may often be exaggerated by the patient himself, since in describing his feelings he is already prone to the kind of distortion or overemphasis of the negative that is characteristic of depression. For the same reason, it is rarely possible to predict whether an individual will become depressed after a particular life event. Different people react differently to the same sort of stress—and this indicates that biologic or temperamental factors, already present in a person *before* the precipitating life event occurs, must play a role in his reaction.

The reverse is also likely to be true, as I was eventually to discover for myself. Biologic depressions usually have some reactive factor in them—some life event, however hidden, that contributed in some measure to the onset of the depressive illness.

Actually, what is most significant in the diagnosis and treatment of depression is not so much whether it is a reactive or a biologic depression—both respond to correctly selected antidepressant medication—but the *degree of severity of the depressive symptoms.* In a reactive depression, symptoms are generally less severe and do not as markedly interfere with a patient's general functioning. Treatment need not be as radical, nor is the depression likely to last as long. Grief, after all, usually cures itself within a period of six months, and an obvious precipitating factor such as the loss of a wife or child or parent may indicate that the depression is a normal grief reaction rather than an actual depressive illness.

How is one to tell? A doctor can obviously not in all cases wait six months to see whether a depression will pass of its own accord; he has to make up his mind more quickly than that. At the present state of knowledge, a summing up of all the symptoms appears to be the best indicator of the severity of a depression, rather than individual symptoms considered in isolation. To assist the doctor in making his diagnosis, questionnaires have been developed with rated answers that establish the severity of symptoms with considerable accuracy. Such depression rating scales are also useful guides for following the course of a depression and evaluating the results of therapy.

What is more critical than the differentiations made between various kinds of depression is the fact that different kinds of depression may react differently to different forms of treatment. In practice, this inevitably involves a period of trial and error, with various kinds of antidepressant drugs as well as psychotherapy and close observation of the patient's finer gradations of reactions: as time goes on, the doctor will note that one antidepressant will show better results, with fewer side effects, than another. How to choose the optimal drug at the start of treatment is one of the more challenging aspects of current research in the field of antidepressant drugs.

During our interview, Dr. Weissman described for me a considerable body of scholarly literature on depression, some of it going back to the writings of the ancient Greeks and Romans. Perhaps the best summary of the history of depression is to be found in *A History of Medical Psychology,* by that extraordinarily well-rounded man of medicine and letters Dr. Gregory Zilboorg. Sigmund Freud, who wrote about depression in his essay "Mourning and Melancholia" (among other writings), felt it was a result of hostilities turned inward. "However," Dr. Weissman added brightly, "we've found that our patients seem to have everything *but* repressed hostility." Dr. Freud, I felt, was wrong on that one.

The more she talked, the more fascinated I became. Obviously, there was a great deal going on here. I heard names that hitherto had been only meaningless labels

I encountered from time to time in news stories. There was the National Institute of Mental Health in Washington, a division of the Department of Health, Education and Welfare. It had a Psychopharmacology Research Branch, headed by Dr. Jerome Levine, which specialized in aiding the research being conducted in many different places and countries on antidepressant drugs. The very word "psychopharmacology" is an entirely new one in the dictionary of medical terms, describing as it does a branch of research into the biochemical aspects of mental illness that did not even exist some twenty years ago. I heard of the National Association for Mental Health, with a country-wide membership of about one million people, which is engaged in fund raising, volunteer work and lobbying for the aid of the mentally ill.

As for the Depression Research Unit, in whose offices I now sat, Dr. Weissman described it as being primarily involved in clinical research from which it might eventually be possible to determine the most effective ways of treating the various kinds of depression. Associated with the Connecticut Mental Health Center, a block away, and with the Yale University Department of Psychiatry, the Unit was conducting research on depressed outpatients who came from in and around New Haven. Every step of the treatment of every patient was noted and filed. Patients' names and any identifying information were omitted to ensure absolute confidentiality. The statistics included reports on patients who were "randomized" after three months of treatment—i.e., some were kept on regular medication while others were given placebos (pills disguised as antidepressant medication but actually containing no drugs at all). The purpose of placebos was to determine the degree to which patients respond psychologically to medication that they believe is helping them. This is a standard technique in medical research because all human beings are to some degree affected by the power of suggestion.

Out of all this would eventually come the answers to some basic questions: Which is most effective in the treatment of depression—medication or therapeutic counseling? Or perhaps a combination of both? How long should treatment be continued after the symptoms have been brought under control? What is the most effective form of maintenance treatment? Should patients be kept on drugs for a certain period of time and then allowed to taper off? And if so, should they continue for some time thereafter with psychotherapy alone? Or should the entire treatment be a combined effort utilizing drugs *and* psychotherapy?

Finding the answers to such questions and thereby defining and establishing effective maintenance treatment programs was considered by Dr. Weissman to be one of the more important jobs the Depression Research Unit was doing. "If we were interested only in relieving a patient's symptoms," she said, "we could shake hands and wish him good luck at the end of the treatment period. But that is really only the beginning. We see our job as going much further than that. We want to find out how to *maintain* the mental health of our patients after they have been successfully treated and have gone home to life situations that do not basically change."

In other words, a housewife with five growing children and an alcoholic husband—the kind of situation that in one form or another has driven thousands of women into depressions they can neither cope with nor understand—such a housewife might, with luck, find her way into a community mental health center, might be hospitalized for a time or, if possible, treated on an outpatient basis; and eventually she would emerge from her treatment feeling her old self again. But once she got home, her children would still come weeping to her with their problems, her husband would still come home drunk every Friday or Saturday night, and the budget would still not stretch enough to cover all the things needed to keep the household functioning. How long before the budget of her mental resources would be shot to hell again? How long before she would collapse once more under the pressures of an intolerable everyday existence? How could she be helped to meet those pressures, given the circumstances of a life that could not basically be changed?

Such answers are not easy to come by. It requires the evaluation of hundreds of cases, each one with its own particular variation of human problem and human psyche, to make any meaningful generalizations upon which an effective maintenance program might be built. Women are different from men; older women are different from younger women; the menopause plays its own particular role in shaping a woman's psychic destiny; and it is even possible that men undergo a metaphoric "male menopause," which can trigger a depression. There is the "empty nest syndrome," which often seizes the parents in a happy family when all the children have grown up and gone away to take up their own lives. There is the time of retirement, when men or women who all their adult lives have functioned effectively in a career are told, in effect: Age has rendered you useless; it is time for you to go. What is a man or a woman to do with a life that is suddenly empty of the job that for so many years gave meaning to each working day?

So far, the Depression Research Unit has established reliable medical data to cover an eight-month maintenance period. This may not seem much, considering the nearly eight years that the Unit has been gathering statistics, but it is in fact a very considerable achievement. The data clearly show the value of antidepressant drugs in relieving symptoms, and indicate possible side effects 66 for each type of drug. The material establishes the value of concurrent psychotherapy in helping patients to adjust to their life situations. It outlines a method of treatment: drugs first, until the patient can function well enough to discuss rationally his life and his life situation; then a combination of drugs and psychotherapy until the root causes of the depression have been exposed and dealt with and the symptoms have been brought under firm control.

All this is, so far, for the short term of eight months maximum. What about the long term? A lifetime, say? Nobody knows as yet. The studies are incomplete, the material is not available, adequate data are lacking.

But it is now known that relapses can be dealt with reliably. This is of the greatest importance, since depression is so often a recurring illness.

The word "reliable" bears some discussion. It is a big word in medicine. "Reliable" means something that is effective for you and for me, and for the elderly neighbor down the street and the wild kid across town who every so often goes on unaccountable rampages in the grief and distress of an adolescent depression. Before a medical researcher will use the term "reliable" to describe a method of treatment, it must be checked and rechecked in every conceivable kind of way. There is, for example, the "double-blind" test, in which both a drug and a placebo, identical in appearance, are given to the doctor, who does not know which is which when he administers it to his patients. The effects of suggestion are thus ruled out, and the true efficacy of the medication alone decides the issue. This procedure is fully explained to the patient, who must agree to it before the procedure is undertaken. Only the researcher who keeps track of the pills can evaluate the results of such a double-blind test.

Some doctors believe—and with reason, in some cases —that simply giving a patient a pill automatically makes him dependent on it, reducing his own motivation to try and help himself while increasing his passivity toward his situation, all of which has a negative effect on psychotherapeutic treatment. Others maintain that antidepressant drugs, by relieving a patient's symptoms, make him more accessible to psychotherapy, increase his optimism about his chances of getting well, and thereby increase his motivation to help himself in every way possible. Each theory has its validity, but a way must be found to establish which applies in each individual case so that the proper treatment may be used from the start.

Nobody as yet talks about "cures." It is really impossible for a conscientious doctor to talk about "curing" depression. Is a diabetic ever "cured" of diabetes? No. His symptoms are relieved by constantly taking insulin, but deprived of insulin he will go into shock and die. Therefore he accepts the necessity of taking insulin all his life in order to stay alive. The symptoms are controlled, but the condition is not cured.

At this time, nobody is prepared to say that a person suffering from a depressive illness will have to take antidepressant pills for the rest of his life. Medical science simply doesn't know. I have been taking antidepressant pills for about two and a half years. That is a long time, but the amount I take was tapered off well over a year ago to a minimal dosage. I take my pill as automatically as I brush my teeth before going to bed, and for all I or anyone else knows, I may have to take it until I die. I stopped once, felt symptoms of a relapse after about two weeks, and thereupon started again. The symptoms disappeared within a week. Meanwhile, the psychiatrist I see occasionally in New Haven for a check on my condition is following this personal "experiment" with every bit as much interest as I.

Perhaps the best news of all about depression—and all other forms of mental illness as well—is that the attitude of Americans toward these difficult and distressing diseases of the mind has undergone a fundamental change in recent years. Since 1963, when the first Community Mental Health Center was opened in the United States, increasing numbers of Americans have been facing up to the problem of mental illness and accepting the fact that mental patients are not pariahs to be shunned or locked away but people who need medical treatment. Even the language is changing. Such terms as "loony bin," "nut house" and even "crazy" —all pejorative and all common in my youth—are gradually disappearing, and in their place is growing understanding for the problems of the mentally ill and their families.

A great deal of this is due to the simple fact that Community Mental Health Centers—more than five hundred of them at this writing—now exist all over the country, not only serving the mentally ill but also promoting the idea that mental illness is a human problem that requires human help. In addition, there are more than a thousand divisions and chapters of the National Association for Mental Health country-wide, all with extensive educational and volunteer programs that help to combat unjustified fears and superstitions about mental illness and bring aid and comfort to the afflicted in the hospital, the Center and the home.

The Community Mental Health Center program is in itself a revolutionary idea. Its objectives are to bring psychiatric care to the community, to combat ignorance of mental health problems, to make effective psychiatric care available and accessible to all on the same basis as physical medical care. All that a patient has to do is walk into a Community Mental Health Center and explain his problem. The Center fulfills the five basic requirements of providing (1) inpatient care; (2) outpatient care; (3) an emergency room to treat urgent cases; (4) consultation on mental health problems for all who seek help; (5) a direct link to a hospital for those who need it.

The importance of these community centers to the

more remote areas of America is almost incalculable. Far removed from any major city that could provide some form of psychiatric care, beset with fears and doubts about the wisdom of seeking help, persons with serious mental problems such as depression have hitherto been left entirely on their own to cope not only with their illness but with the hostility and ignorance of the community and, in many cases, even their own families. When the fifteen hundred Community Mental Health Centers that the program calls for have been set up and are operating sometime within the next few years, this type of suffering will be, in most of America, greatly reduced.

I have seen these Centers in operation. I have talked with student volunteers of high school or college age who spend from one to three afternoons a week visiting mental patients in hospitals or at home, giving them a chance to talk about themselves, give voice to their fears and receive the kind of reassurance and comfort that I never knew was available. It is difficult for me even to imagine what it would have meant had some such young person come to visit me when I was alone and desperate in my little attic room. It is certainly not too much to say that these volunteers are saving lives, and that the Community Mental Health Centers are rescuing countless Americans from the sort of hopelessness that can only be alleviated, it seems to the victim, by suicide.

What I learned in New Haven opened my eyes to an entirely different world for the mentally ill from the one I had previously imagined. It was a world of hope rather than despair. And what I was about to learn in my further research into the history and treatment of depression was more hopeful still.

More than two thousand years ago in ancient Greece, the physician Hippocrates first classified the symptoms of depression. Today this remarkable man is known as the "father of medicine" in the Western world, and no one is more deserving of the title. He was a keen clinical observer who used the patient as his laboratory, in the best modern tradition, and the symptoms that he noted for depression are so clearly defined they could be used today. It might even be said that he was on the right track in his efforts to determine the cause of the disease. He knew that the seat of the mind lay in the brain, and he attributed melancholia—his name for depression, which I consider a more descriptive one than ours—to an imbalance in the body fluids, specifically to an excess of the "black bile."

Today we know that a chemical imbalance is the chief physiological cause of depression; but chemistry, of course, had not yet been invented when Hippocrates was practicing. His pharmacopoeia was made up of what nature provided in the way of herbs and minerals, some of which have survived even the changes wrought by progress—with refinements, of course. In Hippocrates' day, for example, doctors used to send their mental patients to take the waters of certain hot springs in the north of Italy. When these springs were analyzed in modern times, they were found to contain high concentrations of lithium. This realization is what led to the use of lithium carbonate in the treatment of bipolar—or manic—depression, today, as effective now as it was two thousand years ago.

But despite the hit-or-miss methods that characterized the treatment of depression down through the centuries, nobody could pinpoint the causes or find a reliable treatment. Depression and all other forms of mental illness continued to be looked upon with fear and loathing because of the aberrant behavior they often caused. It was not until the mid-1950s—barely a generation ago —that a real breakthrough was made. It came, as sometimes happens in medicine, accidentally.

Two new drugs were then being introduced into medicine—one for the treatment of hypertension, or high blood pressure, the other to combat tuberculosis. Neither ailment had anything to do with depression, but both medications were observed to have interesting side effects that clearly bore upon the patients' mental states. The antihypertensive drug appeared to produce severe depressions in many of the patients on whom it was used; the drug for tuberculosis seemed to have the opposite effect, inducing extreme euphoria and even mania.

The drug used for hypertension was reserpine, a derivative of the rauwolfia family of herbs, with which Hippocrates would no doubt have been familiar—they have been used in medicine for at least three thousand years for ailments ranging from insomnia to snakebite. The tuberculosis drug was based on the monoamine oxidase inhibitors, substances in the brain of which we shall hear more later.

Repeated clinical tests were made on both animals and humans, and although the picture was not entirely clear, there was little doubt that in many cases reserpine did induce drowsiness, withdrawal and depression, while the MAOIs (as the monoamine oxidase inhibitors were called) made many of the subjects treated euphoric. The question naturally arose: might these observations have some bearing on depression and the manic depressive cycle?

They did. Now it remained to find out why.

One of the scientists who was deeply involved in this early research was Dr. Joseph J. Schildkraut, now a professor of psychiatry at Harvard Medical School. Dr. Schildkraut is today one of the world's leading experts on depressive illness and he has written extensively on the subject. While his scholarly papers are directed to colleagues in the field, with a terminology that is usually beyond the layman's grasp, it is nonetheless instructive to read certain excerpts, which give some idea of how successful medical research has been in this area.

"During the past decade," Dr. Schildkraut wrote in 73

the *American Journal of Psychiatry* in 1965, "there has been a gradual accumulation of evidence suggesting a possible link between the affective disorders (depressions and elations) and changes in central nervous system catecholamine metabolism. . . . These studies have shown a fairly consistent relationship between drug effects on catecholamines, especially norepinephrine, and affective or behavioral states. Those drugs which cause depletion and inactivation of norepinephrine centrally produce sedation or depression, while drugs which increase or potentiate brain norepinephrine are associated with behavioral stimulation or excitement and generally exert an anti-depressant effect in man."

These are fairly deep waters for the layman to wade through, but one clear fact emerges: a link had been discovered between depression, the illness, and certain things that went on in the brain. Let us try to penetrate and clarify this explanation further, for herein lies the salvation of the person suffering from mental depression.

Consider the brain as an organ that operates basically on a system of signals and responses. Physical signals come in constantly from all parts of the body, conveying the senses of touch, sight, sound, hearing and smell. They travel along the nerve fibers in minute bursts of electricity, each burst triggering a tiny squirt of fluid from the nerve endings onto the next nerve cell, or neuron, which in turn fires that cell, and so on to the brain. Here the signals are received by the brain cells, which analyze them and send suitable responses back to the original site.

Thus the prick of a pin on a fingertip sends a pain signal to the brain; there the signal is analyzed and, almost instantly, the response goes back: get that finger away from the pin! This happens so fast that we are unaware of it—the prick, the pain and the jerk of the finger away from the pinpoint seem simultaneous.

But if something goes wrong somewhere along the

route of this elaborate and delicate circuitry, the response may be delayed, or distorted, or it may not take place at all. If Novocain has been injected into the finger, the nerve fibers are temporarily deadened, the signal comes into the brain cells only faintly or not at all, and the finger may be probed at will by a needle or scalpel.

The same sort of thing can happen with signals that have to do with moods or emotions. A joyful event sends a signal for which the response is delight. A threat signals fear; the response is sudden tension and alertness. For each kind of mood there are signals and responses, possibly far more complex than those of the senses, but essentially working in the same way. Bright sunlight in a clear blue sky makes us feel good; gray skies often make us feel downcast; howling winds, thunder and lightning make us afraid.

And as with the analogy of the finger and the pinprick, something can go wrong with the circuitry that transmits moods and the response becomes inappropriate. A depressed person looking out at a sunny day may still feel depressed; gray skies and rain may deepen this depressed mood to the point of complete withdrawal. In a different vein, a manic person may react to a severe thunderstorm with wild and uncontrollable elation, striving to outdo the violence of nature with violence of his own making—howling, shrieking and breaking things.

What goes awry? Why is it impossible to lift a depressed person out of his despair even on days when everything is really going right for him?

Nobody knows for sure as yet; medical scientists, with good reason, are among the most cautious and conservative people in the world. But the answer may lie in that "possible link between the affective disorders (depressions and elations) and changes in central nervous system catecholamine metabolism."

What are the catecholamines? I described above the 75

way in which each burst of electricity, traveling through a nerve cell, or neuron, triggers a tiny squirt of fluid from the nerve endings which causes the next neuron to fire in the same way, releasing another squirt of fluid in turn—ultimately carrying the signal all the way to the brain. Catecholamines are among the families of very complex chemical substances which are released from the nerve endings and which carry out very specific functions in the transmission of impulses from certain nerve endings to other neurons. These substances are called neurotransmitters. Among the catecholamines are two—norepinephrine and dopamine—which appear to play a role in determining a person's capacity to experience feelings of vitality, drive, ambition, pleasure, satisfaction—all the various things that make up what doctors call a person's "affective state." A third neurotransmitter, which belongs to a chemically different family, the indoleamines, is called serotonin, and has also been linked to depressive disorders. Other neurotransmitters may eventually be added to this list.

In the brain, these substances function in microscopic areas at the minute gap between the nerve endings of one neuron and the next neuron in line, which is known as the synaptic cleft. Into this cleft are discharged the neurotransmitters that do the work of passing the signals along. It is the completion of this process which is thought to bring about regulation of changes in a person's mood—and if the quantities of neurotransmitters are out of balance, the mood response will be inappropriate.

To put it this way is an oversimplification for the sake of trying to explain a highly complex function. There are millions of neurons within the brain, which act in different ways; which ones transmit emotions, or how they do it, cannot be said with any degree of certainty. This type of research involves working backward from effect—a depressed or elated mood—to cause. But it is thought that in certain areas of the brain there are collections of neurons and nervous pathways that mediate what we call emotion.

The difficulties hampering this kind of research into the chemical components and functioning of the brain are enormous. The synaptic cleft itself is inaccessible to any kind of probing in a living human being; it can only be seen under a powerful microscope. The quantities of neurotransmitters that function there are even more minute. The only known way of tracing them is by examination of the spinal fluid, the blood and the urine of patients, in which minute amounts are excreted and can be measured.

Studying the changes in norepinephrine metabolism in depressed patients, for example, Dr. Schildkraut and others found a significant correlation of factors. Dr. Schildkraut described it to me: "The excretion of 3-methoxy-hydroxyphenylglycol, or MHPG, as it is known —the major metabolite of norepinephrine in the brain —appears to be relatively low during periods of depression and relatively high during periods of hypomania (as compared to levels during periods of normal affective state) in patients with bipolar manic-depressive disorders. But MHPG excretion does not appear to be comparably reduced in all types of depressive disorders. Such differences in MHPG excretion may possibly provide a biochemical basis for classifying the different types of depressive disorders and for predicting the differential responses to one or another form of treatment."

In other words, doctors now stand on the threshold of a major breakthrough in the treatment of depressive illness: to be able to make clear-cut diagnoses of the *type* of depressive illness which is afflicting the patient, and to be able to prescribe a known and proven medication to combat the depressive symptoms.

Judged by these findings, and by the continuing pa- 77

tient work of scientists like Dr. Schildkraut, Dr. Nathan S. Kline and Dr. Gerald E. Klerman, founder of the Depression Research Unit, depression appears to be linked with a deficiency of norepinephrine and serotonin in the area of the synaptic cleft. Reserpine—the antihypertensive drug that was observed to produce depression—seems to reduce the amounts of the neurotransmitters norepinephrine and serotonin available in the area of the synaptic cleft. This was established by keeping track of the amounts of both substances through analysis of urine, blood and cerebrospinal fluid.

By contrast, the administration of the MAOI types of drugs—the monoamine oxidase inhibitors—appeared to be linked to an *increase* in the amount of available norepinephrine. The tentative conclusion may be drawn that an overabundance of this substance in the area of the synaptic cleft leads to euphoria or mania.

These two basic observations have led to the development of a whole line of new antidepressant drugs, which fall into two main classifications. Both are based on a *reverse* action to that produced by reserpine: i.e., they *increase* the supply of norepinephrine—and in some cases serotonin—in the area of the synaptic cleft. They do this in two ways:

1. Under normal conditions, an enzyme called a monoamine oxidase acts as a corrective brake on the production of norepinephrine in the area of the synaptic cleft. In other words, the monoamine oxidase *inhibits* the production of norepinephrine beyond a certain level in order to keep the system in balance. In a patient suffering from depression, too little norepinephrine may be produced or too much norepinephrine may be inactivated; in either case the supply falls off and the patient becomes depressed. The MAOI types of drugs—the monoamine oxidase inhibitors—put a brake on the brake, so to speak, allowing more norepinephrine to be produced and be available for action.

2. The other types of drugs, the so-called tricyclic anti-depressants, work directly on the circulation of norepinephrine in the area of the synaptic cleft. A certain amount of norepinephrine is constantly being taken back up into the neuron from the synaptic cleft. If too little is discharged into the synaptic cleft or too much is taken up and stored, then the amount of effective norepinephrine available for neurotransmission is decreased, and depression may result. By slowing down or blocking entirely the uptake of norepinephrine into the neuron, the amount that is active in the area of the synaptic cleft is increased, and the depressive symptoms may be relieved.

Of course, cause and effect in medicine are never as simple as described here, but the weight of the evidence now seems to indicate that this is the way things may work. Certainly, the antidepressant drugs are startlingly effective for a great many people, as they were for me. Of the two types of drugs, the tricyclics are generally preferred because the MAOIs may have potentially disturbing side effects that require persons taking them to observe certain dietary restrictions.

It is also interesting to note that the effect of the new antidepressant drugs appears to be closely similar to that of electroshock therapy, which was for many years —and still is, in some cases—the preferred treatment for depressive illness. The passage of an electric current through the brain also seems to have some effect on the metabolism of norepinephrine, and thereby results in relief of the depressive symptoms.

Another drug, lithium, which does not belong in the above classifications, is emerging as an increasingly important factor in the treatment of manic-depressive illnesses. Lithium is chemically related to sodium, potassium, magnesium and calcium, all of which occur in the body and are involved in many different biochemical and physiological processes. It has been speculated that lithium might exert its effects on man- 79 ic-depressive illnesses by displacing or replacing one or another of these substances. Another possibility is that lithium may work in a directly opposite way from the tricyclic antidepressants—decreasing the release and increasing the reuptake of norepinephrine.

In any case, there is no longer any doubt as to the effectiveness of lithium in treating the manic phase of the manic-depressive cycle, and there is reason to hope that it may prove to be a useful drug in treating unipolar depression as well. In cases of manic depression, it has decreased the average relapse rate of a large group of patients under study from once every eight months to once every five years.

Part of this story I learned from Dr. Mason De La Vergne at the Depression Research Unit, part of it from Dr. Klerman, who is now the head of the Erich Linde-man Mental Health Center in Boston, and part of it from Dr. Julian Lieb, the current director of the Dana Psychiatric Division of the Yale–New Haven Medical Center. Dr. Schildkraut also explained to me some of the details, many of which I had previously read in the numerous scholarly papers written on the subject by himself and Dr. Kline. I also added enormously to my background information on depression by reading histories of this disease. Certain men from times long past who fought ignorance, superstition and fear in their efforts to help the mentally ill came to life in my mind as I read— Hippocrates, for example, who was the first to recognize that the center of the mind and of all reason lay in the brain. In his day, Hippocrates risked scorn and even punishment by inveighing against the belief that epilepsy was a curse inflicted by the gods—the reason epilepsy was known in his time as the "sacred disease." He traced the cause of epilepsy, quite correctly, to the brain.

As I read about Hippocrates I came to feel as though I had known him rather well. In my mind's eye, during the time when I was ill, he became a sort of father figure

Two Way Street
Coffee House

Downer's Grove

to me—the personification of the wise old doctor whom I had sought vainly and so often in psychiatrists' consulting rooms. He had a strong personality, which shone undimmed through his writings, and he had no patience with the medical claptrap of his day. Furthermore, he was well aware, as doctors are now, of the potentially fatal outcome of depression: suicide.

Another figure from the past, who captured my imagination even more powerfully, was Paracelsus, the sixteenth-century Swiss physician, who spoke out so bravely against the medical chicanery of his day, and in particular against the witchcraft trials of the Holy Inquisition, which were then ravaging Europe. Paracelsus was, like Hippocrates, a man of strong principles, and one of his most stubborn convictions was that many of those who were accused of having sold themselves to the devil were not possessed at all, but were mentally ill. This got him into a good deal of trouble, and despite his often brilliant insights and the amount of practical medical knowledge that he amassed, he spent most of his life in bitter conflict with his fellow physicians and the authorities, and in consequence died in poverty, still reviled by the members of his profession.

Paracelsus became extremely real to me. The picture I had of him was based on the memory of a beloved schoolteacher, himself a rugged, uncompromising and extremely gifted Swiss, who influenced me greatly in my adolescent years. When a man is researching a subject in an effort to save his sanity, as I was, perhaps his imagination becomes hypersensitive. In any case, it happened that one afternoon, after long hours of reading in the library of Connecticut College in New London, I had a clear vision of Paracelsus coming down the aisle to talk with me. I may have dreamed it; but what is important about this incident is the very sound advice he gave me, which I followed.

"The best laboratory of disease in man is man himself," he told me. "If you have had this disease of melancholia, then you must know its symptoms. You must be able to chart its progress, as it progressed with you. You must be able to find its causes, in yourself. *You* are the laboratory—*you!* Look at *yourself!* Get away from books! They will tell you nothing that you cannot find out better in yourself, in your own experience! Remember—science is *experience!"*

I put the books away then and went home. I knew, with perfect certainty, what I had to do. The old man had shown me the way.

It was not long after this strange encounter that I saw my own psychiatrist for the last time. It took an act of will to break the routine, but the words of Paracelsus were in my mind when I drove beneath the colorful trees of autumn to his house and decided I would end my visits with this one. He was simply not the man I needed. When my fifty minutes were up, I turned my back on his little gray house for good, and the next morning I called up the Depression Research Unit in New Haven.

Within a week, I was sitting in front of Dr. De La Vergne in the familiar run-down brick tenement.

"Dr. De La Vergne," I said, "would it be possible for you to take me on as a patient?"

He studied me with his deep-sunk dark eyes. He showed no trace of surprise, only warm sympathy.

"What is your trouble?"

I told him the whole story. He took notes and asked questions. Finally, he asked to see the medication I had been taking, and I gave him the bottle.

He looked at it for a moment, then asked:

"And how much of this are you taking?"

I told him. He sighed. "Ah, well," he said, "it's an old story to us. You ought to be taking a much larger dose. Most doctors simply don't know enough about these new antidepressant drugs. They are afraid of side effects and so they consistently underdose their patients. I only wish you had come to me sooner; we could have had you feeling better a long time ago."

When I left New Haven a short while later, I had two new prescriptions in my pocket. "Don't expect anything to happen right away," Dr. De La Vergne warned me. "This medication has a cumulative effect—it has to build up to a certain level in your bloodstream before you will notice any change. This usually takes a week to ten days. Come and see me a week from now, and let's see how you feel then."

Within a week the miracle began to happen. What I remember specifically is waking up one morning feeling *good*. I had had a deep, completely restful night's sleep of about eight hours. No disturbing dreams. No three-o'clock awakening. No fears, no worries, no guilt feelings. I looked out of my window at a gray November day and I thought I had never seen a more beautiful world. For the first time in more than a year I felt *good!*

That was how it began. My dominant memory is of those marvelous nights when, night after night after night, I fell quietly asleep, slept deeply without awakening, and woke up in the morning feeling at peace with the world. There even came a time when as soon as I awakened, I began to look forward to the moment when I would sink back into sleep that evening.

This happened in November 1971. I began work that fall on a new book about the North Woods for the Time-Life series on the American Wilderness. The book took me far afield, on journeys lasting two or three weeks, deep into Minnesota and the far northern reaches of Canada. I tramped the woods and the tundra in temperatures ranging down to forty degrees below zero, on snow that in the open was packed as hard as cement by the wind and in the sheltered places of the forest was up to my eyes and as soft as powder. I slept in strange places—in tents, in trains, in primitive motels in legendary villages of the Far North like Fort Chipewyan on Lake Athabaska and Fort Smith on the Slave River. Sometimes in the night I awoke and heard the lonely sound of wolves howling from the wilderness beyond my bed, and huskies replying from the Indian dwellings round about. But never did I awaken to the fear-ridden nightmares I had known for so long.

There is little doubt that I had been suffering from a norepinephrine imbalance, which the antidepressant medication had now set aright. What caused this imbalance, or what specific kind of depression I suffered from, I do not know, for such matters are still the subjects of intensive and highly complex research and debate. But I do know now that, for whatever reasons, I had been mentally ill, and quite desperately so. As Dr. Hugh Storrow of the University of Kentucky has written:

"Depression probably causes more human suffering than any other single disease—mental or physical. Only schizophrenia causes more initial admissions to mental hospitals. More important is the fact that there are probably five times more depressed patients than schizophrenics walking the streets and sitting in physicians' waiting rooms. Furthermore, depression is one of the few psychiatric illnesses with a significant mortality rate. There are 20,000 known suicides a year in the United States. . . . One expert estimates that two million persons in this country make at least one attempt at self-destruction each year. All of these people are seriously troubled, and many of them are depressed."

But I was out of it at last; my season in hell seemed to be over. Yet a question still nagged at me: Was it *really* over? Was there still something buried in my unconscious mind, some event, some unanswered question that might arise to plague me in years to come?

It was some time before I found the answer. There did

not seem to be any way in which I could willfully pursue it; I had long since explored every avenue I knew of that led to my subconscious and its buried memories of times long past. Therefore I forgot about it for a while, and tried instead to review the course of my illness, to absorb what I had learned about depression, to find a place for this extraordinary experience within the context of my life.

9

What had I learned—not just about depression, but about myself?

Positive things first. I was a very different person from the man who had come to this seaside village from Paris. I had gained immeasurably from the journey into self that my depression entailed. I had more depth, more compassion—about myself and toward my fellow man. I had learned a great deal about the human psyche and the strange ways in which it works. I felt better equipped to meet the stresses of living in an unsettled world, and better able to understand the motivations of others around me whose lives affected my own.

Viewed in this sense, the depression I had suffered through was an enriching and rewarding life event.

Digging a little deeper: if my depression had shown me my weaknesses, it also showed me strengths I never knew I had. I marveled at the way, morning after morning, I had got myself out of bed to face a day that seemed to promise only devastation and despair. How did I manage to do it? I had never known I had it in me to fight back in this fashion; mild-mannered by nature, I had always seen myself as a man who did not seek out conflict and, when it was unavoidable, tried to find reasonable ways around it rather than facing it head on.

I remembered the lonely hours I had spent arguing with the dead man in the park, and how my friend Kasimir had reached a helping hand out from the grave to give me courage in this deadly dialogue. I had always admired in Kasimir the indomitable good humor with which he faced and overcame adversity. Now I saw I had some of this courage, too, and I began to look upon myself with greater understanding and esteem.

I also realized for the first time that it was the loss of self-esteem that brought me to my lowest ebb in my depression. Without *some* inner strength, without at least a vestige of respect for himself and what he stands for, a man cannot survive. But to preserve these things he must, in whatever primitive way is open to him, defend himself against his illness. He must break the cycle of his brooding thoughts, and the only way he can do that is to act.

Act? Act how?

Do something, anything. It really doesn't matter 87

what, as long as it is a positive action. And I saw now that I *had* acted thus in my defense: I *had* fought back.

I did this by forcing myself to do three simple things each morning:

1. I got out of bed;
2. I made myself some coffee;
3. I made the bed.

If this sounds too trivial to mention, it is not. It proved to me, day after day, that I was still able to accomplish *something,* even though my mind was telling me I was a total loss. By the act of getting out of bed I proved that I could still command my body and had at least a semblance of free will. By the act of making coffee, I proved that I could still do something to preserve myself and thus deny my growing wish for death. By the act of making my bed I proved that I had not fallen completely into the state of sloth and disarray that my disorganized mind constantly told me I was in; I still cared.

These very small beginnings were extraordinarily important. I realize now that such daily acts—which inevitably led to larger ones, such as going to my office and doing a day's work—were the primitive foundations on which later, with the help of drugs and psychotherapy, I could rebuild my self-esteem.

From a larger point of view, the most important thing that my depression did for me was to make me face the fact that I was mentally ill. For a creature of the twentieth century, Freud and the burgeoning science of psychiatry notwithstanding, this is no small achievement. Mental illness is still one of the great bugaboos of modern man. Never mind all the things we've learned in the last fifty years or so; despite improved attitudes, a lot of people do still look on it with much the same aversion that our forefathers did for five thousand years or more. For them, mental illness still carries a stigma with it.

Why? Is mental illness any different, in a social sense, from a disease of the heart, the lung, the liver or some other vital organ?

Yes, it *is* different—because its very nature affronts mankind. Diseases of the mind may bring with them aberrant behavior that other people cannot understand. The mentally ill sometimes act in weird ways—they howl, they moan, they mutter; or they withdraw completely into some world of their own in which they brood incessantly. They are subject to unpredictable outbursts of temper or violence, or equally unpredictable moods of quiet, desperate weeping in some dark corner. They do not react like "normal" people, and this makes "normal" people afraid.

But we cannot ignore them. They are people like the rest of us—but people who have temporarily (or permanently) lost their way.

Do they even *know* that they are ill? Sometimes yes, often not. I didn't until my doctor told me that I was. Until then, I had lived in mortal fear that I was losing my mind but I did not see myself as ill.

How *can* a person know when he is suffering from depression?

This is a difficult but highly significant question. It suggests an entirely new area of inquiry for the family doctor—one into which some doctors are already venturing, but which many others still ignore. It is all too often true that when a person who is depressed consults his doctor, he does so not because of his depression but because of some somatic—i.e., physical—ailment that may mask his depression so completely that his emotional problems, *which led to his physical troubles in the first place,* pass undetected by the doctor.

Consider once more, with the benefit of hindsight, what happened to me.

Symptoms? There was nothing that prompted me to visit a doctor. I had no fever, nothing hurt, I wasn't nauseated, I ate and my digestion was normal. So what could be wrong with me?

I was tired and sad. I felt friendless and alone. I slept badly and was given to long periods of hopeless brooding. I wept often, by myself, in response to the most trivial happenings. I carried an intolerable burden of guilt, much of it associated with things that had nothing to do with me—like the drug problem or the war in Vietnam. And most of all, I always felt afraid.

But go to a doctor with these things? The thought never entered my head!

The question is extraordinarily difficult because the symptoms, compared to such specific reactions to a physical disorder as pain, fever, nausea and so on, are intangible, wavering, elusive. Very few people are likely to go to their family doctor and say to him, "I don't think anything is really wrong with me; it's just that I feel blue and scared all the time."

Only education can really help here. That is what makes the Community Mental Health Centers so important, and what lends real urgency to the work of such nationwide organizations as the National Association for Mental Health. If people *know* what it means to have sustained feelings of depression, and if family doctors know the right questions to ask when they are faced with such complaints, then a great many cases of depressive illness can be spotted and treated before they become deeply rooted or do lasting harm.

One of the complicating factors in depression is that the mind, even if it is delusional, continues to function in what seems to the patient to be a reasonable and normal way. Some seventy years ago, a man named Clifford Whittingham Beers, a graduate of Yale University and a resident of New Haven, Connecticut, described a particularly striking instance of this in his book *A Mind That Found Itself.* Beers had fallen ill with depression and finally tried to kill himself by jumping out of a third-floor window, an act that led to his being confined to a mental hospital.

"Most sane people," Beers wrote, "think that no insane person can reason logically. But this is not so. Upon unreasonable premises I made most reasonable deductions, and that at a time when my mind was in its most disturbed condition. . . . During the seven hundred and ninety-eight days of depression I drew countless incorrect deductions. But such as they were, they were deductions, and essentially the mental process was not other than that which takes place in a well-ordered mind."

Before the era launched by Sigmund Freud at the turn of the century, no one, doctor or layman, could possibly have understood what was going on in a mind deranged as Beers's mind was, because no one knew anything about the *structure* of the mind. It wasn't even a medical specialty; confinement was the only treatment.

Freud changed all that. Some of his methods and conclusions have now been overtaken by new developments, but there is no arguing the fact that he was the true father of psychiatry, the medical specialty devoted to diseases of the mind, and that he provided the first link between the known physical apparatus of the mind —the nervous system with its impulses and connections with the brain—and the unknown and intangible—the mind itself.

What made this possible were his seminal theories about the structure of the mind.

Freud's earliest intimations of what lay before him came when, as a young doctor still in his thirties, he was working at the Salpêtrière, the great mental hospital in Paris. There he watched hypnosis being used on mental patients. "I received the profoundest impression," he wrote later in his autobiography, "of the possibility that there could be powerful mental processes which nevertheless remained hidden from the consciousness of men."

This was his first encounter with the phenomenon that led to his theory of the "unconscious"—mental processes that function very much like a second mind but are so deeply buried that the patient is completely ignorant of their existence. Even today, some eighty years after Freud published his theories, many people are unaware of their significance or unable to see the ways in which they apply to individual human beings. That, too, is part of the mystique of mental illness. It is much easier to admit the possibility of a serious or even potentially fatal ailment than of mental illness, *which implies a loss of control of self.* To seek psychotherapeutic help is tantamount to admitting that one can no longer control one's own impulses—and too often this is a shameful thought.

Freud's awareness of the role of the unconscious provided the key for understanding the processes that go on in the ailing mind. We all carry within us a great pool of the unknown in which is stored much of the ancient common experience that makes us human beings. And this discovery also suggests an answer to the vital and baffling question of *how* a person becomes mentally ill.

Immediate causes (biochemical, hereditary, traumatic) for the moment apart, a mind is ailing when its unconscious psychological manifestations have become so powerful that they overwhelm the conscious mind and assume the convincing force of reality. When an individual's fantasy world is more real to him than the real world around him, then he needs professional help. And because to the mentally ill the world they are in is the "real" world, however gay or grim it may seem, they often cannot know they are ill.

Thus, also, is borne out Clifford Beers's contention that the mentally ill can reason just as logically as those who are well. *Of course* they can! Their minds are functioning perfectly well—except that they are functioning on false premises. The person who acts depressed does so because he *is* depressed—and never mind telling him that things are not that bad, that he should pull himself together and snap out of it. He *can't* snap out of it because in his world things *are* that bad.

An instance that strikingly illustrates this comes to mind out of my own experience. It happened on the morning of my averted suicide, the morning with which I began this book. I was sitting in my chair waiting for my wife to feed me breakfast when, down the hall, I heard the outside door open and footsteps come toward my room.

I knew with absolutely certainty who it was, as though I could see right through the walls. It was my son returning unannounced from Vietnam, where he had been leading an Airborne Ranger platoon in combat for a year.

If ever there was a situation in which a man would do everything possible to pull himself together, this was it. But although I felt this overwhelmingly, there was absolutely nothing I could do. I sat rooted in my chair and waited, trembling, like a man condemned. I heard the footsteps stop outside the door; I saw the handle turn. I shrieked inwardly at myself: "Get up! *Get up!*" Then he was there.

To me, he looked seven feet tall. The brass on his uniform glittered, the ribbons were flashes of color on his chest, his boots shone like twin mirrors. He was everything I was not—strong, healthy, alive.

His eyes fastened on me and widened in surprise and concern. "My God, Pop!" he exclaimed. "What's the matter with you? You look *awful!*"

That is what depression can do to a man. I don't believe I will forget that moment, or my own dreadful sense of helplessness, until the day I die.

Must everyone be so helpless in the face of a depression? Is there no way that an individual can tell if he is seriously depressed? Is there no way that he, his family or his friends can distinguish between a blue mood and a genuine case of depressive illness?

The best explanation bearing on this central problem 93

that I have encountered comes from Drs. Jonathan H. Pincus and Gary J. Tucker in their book *Behavioral Neurology.* "If the symptoms of depression are *present in mild form and transiently* (not lasting more than six months)," they write, "and follow emotionally charged events (usually loss of job, health or loved one), the reaction may be considered as grief. If the symptoms are severe, regardless of the precipitants, if they persist, and if they interfere with the patient's functioning from day to day, the condition should be regarded as depressive illness and be treated."

It is, of course, as difficult for an individual or anyone around him to assess the severity of his symptoms as it would be for him to assess the severity of a fever or other symptom of somatic illness. In such cases, to be on the safe side, one sees a doctor—and in the same way, a psychiatrist can be consulted by anyone who suspects he may be suffering from a real depression. The doctor might well employ one or another of the several depression-rating scales mentioned in an earlier chapter. As Pincus and Tucker say: "[This] is a relatively reliable method of judging the severity of a depression, following the course of the disorder, and evaluating therapy."

A Community Mental Health Center can help in the same way. If there is one within reach, it requires no more effort than to walk in, explain the problem and discuss it with a specialist. If help is needed, it will be given, and at once; if not, the individual can go home reassured.

Had I known these things that fall after my return from Paris, I would have been spared much agony. Instead I had both the pain of the experience and the benefit of all of the things I learned about depression. There remained only one thing: the nagging feeling I still had that there was something more behind it than a simple biochemical deficiency. I still sought, unconsciously but persistently, for a life event that underlay the biochemical cause and eventually brought about a situation in which the biochemical balance in my brain was disturbed enough for me to fall really ill.

I found it one day almost, it seemed, by accident. It did not appear as a result of further exploration of my memories, nor did it require any intellectual effort on my part. One day it was simply *there,* as though I saw a signpost in my mind.

It lay in the story of a love affair in a war-torn city, long ago.

10

It began with a dream.

By the time of the dream, I was well into this book. Never having written about my own life before, I had not realized how like a deep analysis autobiographical writing can be. Certainly it is equally demanding of the psyche. It is lonely and difficult to put down everything as it really happened; no excuses, no embellishments. The words, the thoughts press unsuspected buttons in the mind as they pass, set reels of memory spinning like tape in a recorder and bring to light faces, events, conversations long since forgotten. But unlike a tape recorder, such thoughts are not easily turned off.

One night, thinking of where I would go next in this book, I had a dream. . . .

When I was stationed in Berlin again just after World War II, I often traveled the autobahn that led westward to the American Zone of Occupation. For some one hundred miles of Russian-occupied Germany this broad, double-lane highway unrolled almost arrow straight to Helmstedt, where there was a Red Army checkpoint, a strip of no man's land, and then an American checkpoint on what is now the frontier of West Germany. After that came the city of Braunschweig, silent, blackened ruins, and not long after that a jagged drop where American bombs, months before, had knocked out a mile-long autobahn bridge across a valley.

A forest of detour signs warned travelers of the autobahn's end and the road, turning suddenly to the left, plunged down a steep embankment into an open field. Tanks, trucks, jeeps and half-tracks had long since chewed it into a crisscrossing maze of deep ruts. When it rained, this became a hopeless quagmire. It was a driving hazard of the worst and most frustrating kind, for there was no other way of getting through to the continuation of the autobahn. Even Army drivers in vehicles with all-wheel drive viewed it with extreme distaste; for civilians like me, if the car got stuck, it was a matter of sitting and waiting until some Army type came along to pull us out.

On this particular night in 1972, my dream was apparently connected in some way with this three-mile detour. I could not remember any of the details, but 97 when I awoke in the darkness before dawn, my mind was on that road and I traveled it again in a sharply etched memory.

It was in the spring of 1947. I was returning to Berlin from a two-week trip to Frankfurt. It was black night outside, and it was raining.

It was foolish to try the detour under those conditions, but I was tired and impatient. Home and bed and wife and family were only about three hours away if I got through. I took the chance.

The detour was in miserable shape. Black water gleamed in countless deep holes in the labyrinth of ruts, reflecting back the white glare of the headlights. The car lurched, twisted, stumbled, splashed as we roared along in low gear, climbing, descending, then climbing again. She was a five-year-old Chevy sedan I had bought used two years before, and the war-torn roads of Germany had already taken twice the toll of her previous existence; she was almost as tired as I.

Still we kept on going through the streaming night, wipers clacking, engine never missing a beat as we rode up and down like a ship riding storm-tossed waves. Then, rounding a curve just below the top of yet another ridge, I came upon a sight that seemed to spell my journey's end.

A two-and-a-half-ton Army truck with a two-wheel trailer hitched on behind had somehow slewed around in the ooze and was now blocking the track. Its nose pointed toward the hilltop, and the trailer hung foolishly on the lip of a plunge into the valley. Three uniformed Americans were circling their six-wheel-drive problem, flashlights stabbing into the gloom as they disconsolately inspected wheels mired to the hub caps.

My Chevy shuddered to a stop. The three GIs looked up in surprise. In the brilliant glare of the headlights the truck seemed as big as a house, and just as immovable. There was no way around it, and there was no way back.

It was three hours before I got out of there.

We all put our backs into the job, shoveling, pushing, digging up rocks to put under the wheels. Some suicidal maneuvering by one of the GIs finally got the truck into a position where the wire cable of the winch mounted on the front bumper could be looped around a tree. Then I got a classic demonstration of what such a winch can do. Slowly it pulled the truck and trailer through the mud up toward the top of the hill. We stopped once and fixed the cable to another tree; now the truck could be turned so that it faced in the direction of the road again. One more tree, and the massive wheels stood on firm ground again at last.

Then it was my turn.

I was drenched, sweating, exhausted and spattered with mud. I got in, started the engine and backed away a little from the gaping, liquid hole the truck had left. Then I floored the accelerator and we roared forward.

Bang! We hit that hole like the *Queen Mary* running full tilt into a tidal wave. The front end plunged in, and a huge dollop of watery mud exploded on the windshield in a blinding smash. The three GIs fell in behind and put their shoulders to the Chevy's shuddering rear. The wheels spun mud at them in a mad deluge; the car lurched on. Now the front end began slowly to rise again. The rear end plunged in, falling as though into a pond, but the old car somehow kept up its forward motion. Engine roaring, soldiers cursing, I screaming, she crawled inch by inch through that awful hole, shaking off mud and water like a plowhorse until at last she emerged on the far side.

We heated up some K-ration coffee then, and sat for a while in the dry, comfortable interior of my car, smoking and talking. Then we shook hands and went on our respective ways.

Within ten minutes, as we shuddered up the last, long hill, my headlights picked out a black-and-yellow sign in the gloom: "BERLIN."

A quarter of a century later, waking in the blackness before a Connecticut dawn, this was the memory that came to me.

Berlin! Except for one brief overnight stop in 1968, when I was on my way to Warsaw, I hadn't been there for twenty years. I had never wanted to go back. Berlin was something very special to me. It was the place from which Hitler had flung the evil scourge of Nazism across half the world. I had seen it happen, and had borne witness to it in the pages of the New York *Times*. But Berlin was also where I had been young, where I had started my career, and where for the first time in my life I really fell in love.

Berlin was the city where some of the most beautiful and most painful events of my life had happened to me. I had long since locked them away in some dusty filing cabinet in my mind.

Did the dream mean I must go back there now? I really did not want to see again that place where once we lived, nor feel again the way we were.

I lay in the dark and tried to close off memory. A church bell chimed the hour—4 A.M. Then, as from a great distance, I heard another, long-forgotten sound. My hackles rose; I groaned and buried my head in the pillow. But the sea breeze carried the sound to me; I could not block it out.

I rolled over, stared into the blackness of the Connecticut predawn, listened and remembered.

It was the sound of air raid sirens. . . .

I was lying on the rooftop of No. 1 Kanonierstrasse, the office of the New York *Times* in Berlin. It was a night in September 1940, in the second year of the war. The blacked-out city lay as still as death. Barely discernible, the buildings across the street loomed against a sky glimmering with stars. Beyond, the Wilhelmsplatz lay bathed in pale starlight, silent and deserted. The lovely old building that now housed the Ministry for People's Enlightenment and Propaganda—the domain of Dr. Joseph Goebbels—gleamed ghostlike on its northern border; diagonally opposite on the western side crouched the fortresslike bulk of Adolf Hitler's new Reichs Chancellory.

The air raid sirens had sounded some ten minutes before. Their wailing cry was always electrifying, and no one in Berlin had yet become accustomed to it. "If so much as a single enemy aircraft crosses the borders of the Reich," Air Marshal Hermann Göring had proclaimed in the early days of the war, "then my name is Meyer!" There had been a lot of bitter jokes about Air Marshal Meyer in the streets of Berlin for some time now. The Royal Air Force, in an astonishing and unexpected show of daring and determination, had roused the resentful Berliners from their beds perhaps a dozen times already and showed no signs of letting up.

My heart was with those pilots up there in the dark and distant skies. With most of Europe helpless under the weight of German occupation and England fighting alone like a cornered bulldog, no one could then foresee the fleets of four-engined Stirling and Lancaster bombers with their huge loads of destruction that within two short years were to devastate the German cities. In the fall of 1940, what was coming over at the western borders of Berlin was a flight of perhaps eight or ten Handley Pages and Wellingtons, twin-engine tactical bombers that could just about reach Berlin with five hundred or so pounds of bombs apiece, and then had to get back to England by the shortest possible route, having no fuel for evasive action. There were no fighter planes to protect them nor radar beacons to guide them; they were entirely on their own. They were a damned nuisance to Berliners, an outrageous embarrassment to Hitler and Göring; and to me the men in those planes were heroes.

Now came the distant crack and boom of antiaircraft

fire. Far off to the southwest over Potsdam, a searchlight suddenly shot up into the black sky; then another, and another. Thin, probing fingers of intense white light, the beams wandered back and forth for a while, searching; then abruptly, one of them wavered and stopped. Instantly the others swept across the sky to join it. The three beams formed a huge tepee of light; and where they crossed, a white speck gleamed like a moth in a flame. All around it the sky became alive with sparkling flashes, and the noise of the guns reminded me of the clusters of firecrackers we used to explode back home on the Fourth of July.

The white moth never wavered. On and on it came, and in the brief instants of silence between the crackling, rolling thunder of the guns I heard its engines' drone, distant and unbearably pathetic. I had a sudden vision of the men in the cockpit, their faces—British faces, perhaps the face of some friend of mine among them—crazily lit by the flashes of the exploding shells, their eyes intent on their instruments as the plane bored on. I lay helplessly on my rooftop and prayed for them.

Then it happened. The white moth disappeared suddenly in the pinprick of a distant flash. Where it had been, a yellow glow boiled slowly up like an exploding star. Above it a puff of black smoke rose skyward. There was a deep, hollow, reverberating boom, and bits of glowing flame drifted earthward like falling leaves, flared briefly and disappeared. No parachutes blossomed in the star-filled sky. The white moth was gone.

Beside me, I heard a sound like a long-drawn sigh. Erich, the little black-haired office boy, was crouched there, his eyes wide and staring. *"Jesses Maria,"* he breathed. "They got him." I turned back and scanned the sky again.

It was quiet for a moment; only the sound of engines droning in the distance. Then, like a silent explosion, the searchlights leaped into the air again and the guns

102

began their crackling noise, much closer now. Again the lights probed the sky. One enormous beam leaped up suddenly from the Tiergarten park, less than half a mile away, incandescent as if some inner fire gave it life. The guns seemed right on top of us now, their flat bangs ringing like the crack of lightning strokes, each with its echoing crackle in the sky high above.

Suddenly, from out of nowhere, there came an eerie, whistling sound that rose to a piercing scream. I had the awful feeling that the sky was falling straight down on us. The noise surrounded us; there was no telling where it came from. Louder—louder; closer—closer. Then, beyond the Chancellory in the Tiergarten, a huge flash and a boom that shook the roof on which we lay. The guns were firing in a mounting chorus now. Crack-*boom!* Crack-*boom!* Crack-*boom!* The sky was alight with their flashing explosions, and dim clouds of smoke rolled up toward the darkening stars.

"Mein Gott!" Erich shrieked suddenly. "Up there! *Look!"*

Caught full in the searchlight's glare, there was a plane. It was so close that I could see the spinning disks of its propellers and the British markings on the fuselage. In the same instant that I glimpsed it, it disintegrated.

There was a sudden, rending, crashing boom that obliterated all the other sounds in that wild sky, and it was gone. A huge black doughnut of smoke coiled up into the night. My ears sang from the explosion; the building trembled. A hail of splinters fell with fierce little impacts all around us, forcing us to the shelter of a wall.

I saw five planes go down that night over Berlin. When the all clear sounded, I got into my car and tried to find them. Police had cordoned off the Tiergarten; driving by, I glimpsed an enormous smoking hole near the old Reichstag building. In Lichterfelde, I was stopped and closely questioned. As I stood there showing my press card, three fire engines roared by. The policeman handed back my credentials. "A plane came down over there," he said, pointing. "It started a fire; that's all."

Back in the office, I wrote my story and telephoned it through to Switzerland. At two in the morning, bone weary and dazed, I crawled into my car again and drove through the blacked-out streets to Bambergerstrasse. The sirens wailed again as I parked the car and entered No. 25.

Upstairs, she had just awakened from sleep with the sirens ringing in her ears. I stood there for a moment looking at her, her dark eyes wide and full of dreams, her dark hair tumbling over the pillow.

"Shall we go down?" I asked. "Jesus, I'm so tired. They got five planes; I saw them fall. . . ."

She reached up her arms to me. *"Viens, chéri,"* she said.

I had met her in 1939, in the first winter of the war. A French girl caught by the outbreak of war when she was visiting in Germany, she was living under the protection of the American embassy, which was representing the interests of France in Germany. She was separated from her husband, who had agreed to a divorce—only to disappear in September into the maelstrom of the war. Now she had no way of knowing where he was, nor whether she was still married to him.

We saw a lot of each other that winter, often meeting in the mornings for a swim at the Olympic pool, followed by lunch and long talks until I had to go to work in the middle of the afternoon. We became friends. We shared many interests; we could talk for hours about books, music, our passionate hatred of the Nazis, about each other, about our hopes for a better world after the war. Sometime that winter we became lovers. She had cooked dinner for me in her small furnished room in the Bambergerstrasse, and after dinner she simply asked if I might like to stay. I knew then that I wanted to stay with her for the rest of my life.

We built a little world together in Berlin in those months of war, and while it lasted it was very beautiful. Surrounded by the enemy, we walled ourselves in and lived from day to day. As we grew to love each other, we ceased to talk about the future. How could we? Our future depended on things far out of our control.

When France fell in June 1940, she was arrested by the Gestapo and sent to an internment camp. I thought at the time that I might never see her again. When I did, after weeks of negotiating with the Gestapo to get her out, she was released into my custody, and from then on, although we could not legally be married, we lived together as man and wife, building the walls of our little world even higher.

There was a fatal flaw in that world which we could not recognize at the time. We did not dare question each other about our feelings for each other. What was real, what was unreal in our fragile world? Lovers need to test each other, to question; they must find out where passion ends and love begins. We could never do that. We were like two people who find each other on a life-raft tossing on a stormy sea. We had only each other to cling to, and had we risked loosening our grip we would certainly have been swept away.

We were always living on borrowed time. The war hung over us broodingly; at any moment it might erupt again and in the ensuing cataclysm we would be torn from each other's arms. Is it any wonder that we tried to ignore it, tried to pretend that in our little world we could live and love as other people could, secure in the knowledge that they would have a whole lifetime together?

What was real, what was unreal? For me, she was as

real as all the world outside, with its jackboots, its Hitler salutes, its crashing bombs, its crackling antiaircraft fire. Yet often, waking in the night and feeling her beside me, I was swept by the aching, hollow fear that she might be gone from me the very next day, that some official somewhere whom I did not even know might on a sudden whim command her elsewhere—to a concentration camp, to a work battalion, back to France, to someplace where she would be lost to me forever.

For all our pretending, we lived in the presence of a sad despair. We clung to each other and in the face of desperate things we reaffirmed our love. But never did we dare to test it to see if it was really love.

When finally we were able to leave Germany, this was the way we continued to live. We stayed confined within our fragile world rather than risk what might happen if we left it. There were separations when I went off for long months as a war correspondent, and if there were cracks when I returned we tried to patch them, to keep out the real world that was impinging upon us, to reaffirm with words and passionate embraces the love that had sheltered us in wartime Berlin.

We did this for thirteen years. Then, in a single gesture, she swept our little world aside and it crashed, tinkling and glittering in a thousand fragmented memories, to the floor. And when I could not put the pieces together again I buried them, locked them away in a secret place in my mind and tried to forget them for all time.

But though she left me to marry another man, the old patterns persisted for many years. What was real, what was unreal about our time together? What was the truth about the life we had built in wartime Berlin?

Unknown to me, these questions were so built into the foundation of my life that as long as they remained unanswered I would never be secure. They were tied to every phase and symptom of my depression, and I realized at last that if I did not face them I would be as vulnerable as I had been before. That was the meaning of the dream that had set my thoughts on the road to Berlin.

But I had never realized the depths at which these answers lay, nor the agony that would be involved in finding them.

I remembered how like a miracle it was to me thirty-five years before when this girl with the calm eyes and slow, sweet smile came willingly into my arms. And I remembered the frightful, angry pain that surged years later, with the knowledge that she had given those same eyes, that same smile, that same warm body which was so miraculously mine to other men. How could she? How *could* she?

Today I am no longer frightened by the answer to that question. Did I not do the same, in distant places, when I was lost and lonely during the war? Did not many, many men and women do the same?

Dorothy Parker wrote a poem about this in World War I, and its poignant final lines have long echoed in my mind:

> Only, for the nights that were
> And the dawns that came,
> When in sleep you turn to her
> Call her by my name.

I could at last face my memories, the nights that were, the dawns that came. I loved her then; I know that now.

But it takes two to tango, and this would not be the first time in history that a man loved a woman who did not love him back. If I was naïve for years about sex, I remained ignorant for even longer years about love. To me its final, culminating, unquestionably affirming act was *making* love, and I thought that to make love, again and again and yet again, strengthened love each time by the act, finally underpinning it all with children and a family.

In this, too, I was not alone.

But because I felt this I also felt, when she left me, that in leaving she was destroying not only the basis of the life we had had together but *my* life. She was destroying everything I believed in, everything I was. She was destroying *me*.

Is this real or unreal? Is it true? Does any human being, man or woman, hold such power over another?

In the depths of my depression I found the answer to that question, too. She was not even in my thoughts when I looked down from the rooftop and contemplated letting myself go over, or counted the pills in the bottle on my bedside table and thought how I would swallow all of them.

She was not; my wife and my children were. My wife and I had built our marriage together in a real world of many people, of doubts and questions, of arguments and making up, of loving and caring and knowing each other's weaknesses as well as strengths. We did not need to build a wall to shelter us from the world outside. We knew the strength of love; in Berlin I had known only how utterly vulnerable it was. That was the weakness of our illusory marriage, and if it had survived by many years the collapse of Hitler's Reich, that made it no less vulnerable to the questions that we never asked but that eventually came.

Well, I had loved her in Berlin. Where did that leave me now?

It left me with a memory of something that had been good, strong and whole unto itself. For the first time in all those years, I knew where I stood. It left me with my manhood unassailed, it restored my worth as a man in my own eyes. My fears were gone, and my guilt, and the sick feeling I had lived with for so long—that somehow I had been ignorant and childish and stupid to put so much into an experience that seemed to count for so little in the end. The knowledge that I had loved her made me whole.

Epilogue

When I finished writing the preceding chapter about Berlin, I felt as though I were returning from a long, long journey back to a house that had become strange to me. So lost had I been in the past that I gazed around at the study in which I had been working daily for almost a year, at the faces looking down at me from photographs on the shelf above my desk, at the childish paintings that smiled at me from the walls, and tried to remember where I was.

What was real, what was unreal? Standing on the shadow line of consciousness, I tried to reconcile the names and faces of the long-dead past with what surrounded me now. And then I realized in a flood of unspeakable relief that I would never in my life have to reconcile past and present again. My life was all of a piece, and in it I was a whole man.

For more than twenty years I had blamed the girl in Berlin for a wanton act that had threatened to destroy me. Grief, pain, rage, despair—they seek an outlet; blame provides a ready channel. I had buried all memories of her. I had shut out the recurring pictures of her wide, dark eyes, her tumbled hair, the warm, quiet smile that had greeted me when I came home at night; but they would not die. Berlin had become a city twice buried for me: I heaped bitterness on its tumbled brick and stone and cursed it for the things it had meant to me.

Only once had I gone back, years later, and it was devastating. A whole new city had arisen out of the rubble of the old one I had known. Everything was different. . . .

Everything? When I returned on that one visit my plane touched down at Tempelhof, the same airport from which she and I had departed almost thirty years before. A taxi driver seized my bags and hurried me through the crowded terminal; the unchanged accent of his Berlin speech unnerved me. That night I stood on the balcony of my room at the Berlin Hilton and looked out across the quiet Tiergarten toward the ruins of the Reichstag building and the Berlin Wall. I smelled the unchanged, old, evocative and homesick smells of long ago, and all of a sudden I collapsed into such a storm of 110 abandoned weeping as I had not known since I was a small child. I wept and wept, and the lights of the city shimmered through my tears like the searchlights and the flak bursts of that time long gone, and in my mind I saw her face again, her upraised arms: *"Viens, chéri."*

I fled Berlin the next day, and I never wanted to see the city again.

Now I was back from another journey there, this time in my mind—and I was well. I had gone back over our life together and asked the questions that we never dared to ask. I realize now how much a part of me it was and is. Our lives are an event entire; we cannot cut a part of them away. Berlin is as much a part of me as the study in which I am now finishing this book; her face, her smile belong to me as much as the faces of my wife and children looking down at me as I write this.

No, I am not a stranger in this house, and I know where I belong. With that knowledge, my last fears have vanished, and I have come to the last words about my season in hell. Downstairs I hear my wife calling, and a child's shout in answer. A fresh wind is blowing from the sea and the sun lies warm on the water. It has been a long journey, but it is over now. I gather my papers together and walk happily down the stairs of my home.

There are many people who have helped me in big and little ways to write this book. Ann Harris, my editor at Harper & Row, gave me invaluable suggestions and advice in editing the manuscript. If Ralph Graves and Tom Hyman at *Life* had not published my original article, there might never have been a book at all; I am grateful for their editorial insight. Dr. Robert Lombardo of Westerly, Rhode Island, first diagnosed my depression; I can't thank him enough. To Dr. Myrna Weissman and Dr. Julian Lieb of New Haven, my gratitude for their patience, understanding and help. Finally, in Bill Perry, of the National Association for Mental Health, I found a lifelong friend whose interest and encouragement while I was writing this book never wavered.

75 76 77 10 9 8 7 6 5 4 3 2 1